Community Organizing Against Homophobia and Heterosexism: The World Through Rainbow-Colored Glasses

Community Organizing Against Homophobia and Heterosexism: The World Through Rainbow-Colored Glasses has been co-published simultaneously as *Journal of Gay & Lesbian Social Services,* Volume 16, Number 1 2004.

Community Organizing Against Homophobia and Heterosexism: The World Through Rainbow-Colored Glasses

Samantha Wehbi, PhD
Editor

Community Organizing Against Homophobia and Heterosexism: The World Through Rainbow-Colored Glasses has been co-published simultaneously as *Journal of Gay & Lesbian Social Services,* Volume 16, Number 1 2004.

Routledge
Taylor & Francis Group
New York   London

First published by

Harrington Park Press®, 10 Alice Street, Binghamton, NY 13904-1580 USA

Harrington Park Press® is an imprint of The Haworth Press, Inc., 10 Alice Street, Binghamton, NY 13904-1580 USA.

This edition published 2012 by Routledge

Routledge
Taylor & Francis Group
711 Third Avenue
New York, NY 10017

Routledge
Taylor & Francis Group
2 Park Square, Milton Park
Abingdon, Oxon OX14 4RN

Community Organizing Against Homophobia and Heterosexism: The World Through Rainbow-Colored Glasses has been co-published simultaneously as *Journal of Gay & Lesbian Social Services*, Volume 16, Number 1 2004.

The development, preparation, and publication of this work has been undertaken with great care. However, the publisher, employees, editors, and agents of The Haworth Press and all imprints of The Haworth Press, Inc., including The Haworth Medical Press® and Pharmaceutical Products Press®, are not responsible for any errors contained herein or for consequences that may ensue from use of materials or information contained in this work. Opinions expressed by the author(s) are not necessarily those of The Haworth Press, Inc. With regard to case studies, identities and circumstances of individuals discussed herein have been changed to protect confidentiality. Any resemblance to actual persons, living or dead, is entirely coincidental.

Cover photograph, International Demonstration at the WCAR (World Conference Against Racism), by Fiona Meyer-Cook

Cover design by Jennifer M. Gaska

Library of Congress Cataloging-in-Publication Data

Community organizing against homophobia and heterosexism : the world through rainbow-colored glasses / [ed. by] Samantha Wehbi.
     p. cm.
    Includes bibliographical references and index.
    ISBN 1-56023-268-4 (alk. paper) – ISBN 1-56023-269-2 (soft : alk. paper)
     1. Homophobia–Prevention. 2. Heterosexism–Prevention. 3. Community organization. 4. Political participation. I. Wehbi, Samantha.
HQ76.4.C66 2003
306.76'6–dc21

2003001805

Community Organizing Against Homophobia and Heterosexism: The World Through Rainbow-Colored Glasses

CONTENTS

ABOUT THE EDITOR

Samantha Wehbi, PhD, is Assistant Professor in the School of Social Work at McGill University in Montreal, Canada. She has an extensive background in activism on a wide range of social justice and human rights issues, including organizing against homophobia and heterosexism. Dr. Wehbi has worked as an Outreach Program coordinator in a women's shelter, as the coordinator of a rape crisis center, and as a program officer in a human rights program. Her teaching, research, and community involvement interests include social justice, principles of community development/social action, and international and anti-oppression social work.

About the Contributors

Keith Goddard, MA, is a musician and composer. He is the Development Director for KUNZWANA Trust (since 1990), a cultural organisation dedicated to the promotion and dissemination of the work of Zimbabwean musicians and instrument makers. He has been active in LGBT politics since 1992. Keith has been Programmes Manager for GALZ since 1997.

Nelly Jitsuya was born in Peru of Japanese descent. She first became involved in the Peruvian feminist movement in 1980 through her activism in the socialist feminist group Mujeres en Lucha (Women in Struggle) and the magazine *Mujer y Sociedad (Women and Society)*. She was co-founder of the women's coffee shop La Otra Cara de la Luna in 1983 and of Grupo de Autoconciencia de Lesbianas Feministas–GALF–in 1984. In the past two years, Nelly has worked as co-editor of the online publications *Boletín Beijing +5* and *DESafíos: Boletín de los Derechos Económicos y Sociales de las Mujeres de la Región Andina (Challenges: Bulletin on the Economic and Social Rights of Women of the Andean Region)* and has collaborated in the bilingual *ALAI Information Bulletin* towards the World Conference Against Racism.

Diane Labelle is a Two-Spirited woman of Mohawk heritage living in the Montreal area. She completed graduate level courses in political science at McGill University, and holds a graduate diploma in education. She presently works as an elementary school teacher and an educational consultant. She is an active member of the Lesbian Mothers' Association of Quebec, and is working on dealing with homophobia in the schools. She and her partner of twelve years are parents to two children: a son aged five and a daughter aged three.

Fiona Meyer-Cook is a Two-Spirited woman of African-Ojibwe (Anishinaabe) and Scottish descent. She supervises students for Project Interaction: the gay, lesbian, bisexual and Two-Spirited resource of the McGill School of Social Work; is a consultant for the Native Women's Shelter of Montreal; and is preparing a document for Concordia University (Montreal, Canada) on Urban Aboriginal Women and Community Economic Development. In August 2001, she represented EGALE (Equality for Gays and Lesbians Everywhere) at the U.N. World Conference Against Racism in Durban.

Omar Nahas is a researcher at the Yoesuf foundation, was born in Damascus-Syria in 1964 and has lived since 1989 in the Netherlands. He studied languages and cultures of the Middle East at the Catholic University of Nijmegen and gay and lesbian studies at the University of Amsterdam. Nahas has written a book and several articles on Islam and homosexuality in Arabic and in Dutch.

Michèle Roy is a community organizer who has been involved in women's activism for several decades. She has worked as the Coordinator of the Quebec Coalition of Women's Health Centres and as the Outreach Worker for the Women's Federation of Quebec. In addition, she has developed and delivered several specialized training programs in feminist intervention at the Université du Québec à Montréal. More recently, she has worked with women's groups as a consultant in Gender and Development for the Canadian Centre for International Cooperation in Guinea Conakry. She is currently the Outreach Worker for the Quebec Coalition of Rape Crisis Centres.

Rebeca Sevilla, born in Peru, is an activist for lesbian and gay rights. She has been involved in diverse organizations, such as leftist parties and the Latin American Solidarity Committee. Rebeca was co-founder of the Grupo de Autoconciencia de Lesbianas Feministas–GALF–in 1984, a member of the *Movimiento Homosexual de Lima* (MHOL, 1986-95) and its publicly lesbian Director (1988-1992), and co-Secretary General of the International Lesbian and Gay Association–ILGA (1992-95). She has played an active role in several regional and global networking initiatives. She participated in the United Nations World Conference on Human Rights (1993) and on Women (1995) and coordinated the Foundation Get Organized (1996-2000). Rebeca has published a number of articles on these topics. She has lived in Amsterdam and Vienna since 1996.

Prior to returning to Asia in 1995, **Chung To** lived in the U.S. for 13 years, where he was active in gay Asian American activism, including being the co-chair of Gay Asian and Pacific Islander Men of New York (GAPIMNY) in 1994. During the past seven years, Chung has been active in the tongzhi movement and AIDS prevention work in Greater China, including co-founding the Chi Heng Foundation and the Tongzhi Conference (an organization that organizes international conferences for tongzhi and supporters). Chung holds a bachelor's degree from Columbia University and a master's degree from Harvard University. He presently resides in Hong Kong.

Samantha Wehbi, MSW, PhD, has a background in activism on a broad range of social justice and human rights issues including organizing against homophobia and heterosexism. Her professional experience includes working as an Outreach Program coordinator in a women's shelter, as a coordinator of a rape crisis centre, and as a program officer in a human rights program. Her professional and voluntary work has been located in diverse cultural contexts including central Africa, the North of Canada, rural communities in Ontario as well as the Middle East, her region of national origin. She is currently Assistant Professor at the McGill University School of Social Work where her current teaching, research and community involvement interests include: social justice, principles of community development/social action; international and anti-oppression social work.

Foreword

This book taps into the tremendous courage which channels energy and commitment towards action for the eradication of homophobia, heterosexism and other forms of oppression. Activist voices in this collection speak from dramatically diverse cultures, sharing their analysis and their experiences about organizing for sexual emancipation. While acknowledging that there is still a considerable distance to travel, each author documents examples of progress towards the transformation of oppressive sexual attitudes, policies and practices within their own region of the world. The book recognizes the complexity and fluidity of intersecting, multiple oppressions which often reinforce sexual and gender oppression. Such intersections provide opportunities, such as those documented in this book, for the development of alliances which are so necessary for long-term social change. Such alliances are timely, in face of top-down globalization, now under challenge by grassroots coalitions aiming for greater democracy and global justice.

This is an honest book, addressing the personal pain experienced by people whose sexuality and gender definitions are attacked by opinion leaders and institutional practices. A parallel process is also documented, namely, the experiences of community organizations and social networks that create liberated spaces for emancipated sexual and gender expressions. As these spaces take root and grow, this book reports on the inevitable backlash, along with the betrayals, surprises and joys that constitute the bumpy road towards social justice.

The authors offer us insights about community organizing against long-standing prejudices and hurtful dogmas. If we are open to these insights, there is much to learn about the barriers and successes experienced by a social movement striving for transformation. But more. This

[Haworth co-indexing entry note]: "Foreword." Carniol, Ben. Co-published simultaneously in *Journal of Gay & Lesbian Social Services* (Harrington Park Press, an imprint of The Haworth Press, Inc.) Vol. 16, No. 1, 2004, pp. xxi-xxii; and: *Community Organizing Against Homophobia and Heterosexism: The World Through Rainbow-Colored Glasses* (ed: Samantha Wehbi) Harrington Park Press, an imprint of The Haworth Press, Inc., 2004, pp. xvii-xviii. Single or multiple copies of this article are available for a fee from The Haworth Document Delivery Service [1-800-HAWORTH, 9:00 a.m. - 5:00 p.m. (EST). E-mail address: docdelivery@ haworthpress.com].

work also challenges us to heed the call for engagement as allies in the struggle to create a better world. Too often, academic scholarship and research still mistakenly strives for the goal of objectivity which equates aloofness with research integrity. The result is a so-called neutrality which, like its "apolitical" counterparts, ends up colluding with the very forces of oppression and exploitation that the research claims to deconstruct.

This book, to its credit, is neither neutral nor "objective." It is engaged. It takes a partisan position in favour of the eradication of homophobia and heterosexism. It strives to illuminate the trials and tribulations of organizing towards this objective. It honours the grit and valour of activists for their leadership in this process. We are invited to join in their vision and by implication, to examine our own attitudes and practices. Do our personal beliefs assist or block movement towards the eradication of these oppressive institutions? Do our political actions assist or block such transformation? Do we, as social service providers, support or hinder such liberation?

To help us on this journey, this book offers much encouragement because we discover in each chapter that there *is* progress towards the required transformation. As such, the book provides a significant resource for social service providers, activists, academics, and anyone else wanting to ally themselves with such progress. This collection helps us to better understand how to engage in sexual and gender emancipation, taking into account the relevant cultural and other factors unique to each situation. It also helps us to pull out the common threads from lessons learned, and to distill them into practical action to support the social progress envisioned in the following pages.

Ben Carniol
May 2002, Toronto
Author of Case Critical *(4th edition)*

Preface

I sat with my friend finishing our coffee and talking about his recent trip back to Egypt. A heavy feeling weighed on both our hearts as we spoke of the recent police arrests of 50 young men "suspected of homosexual acts." Being both of Arab origin and engaged in anti-oppression activism, we understood the ramifications of these arrests in a country where homosexuality is still a crime. More specifically, we both lamented the reluctance of almost all Egyptian human rights groups to take on this case which could potentially tarnish their reputations and jeopardize their bargaining power with the state on other issues. Defying state pressure and intimidation tactics, one Egyptian human rights group accepted the challenge of this case.

Reflecting back on this discussion, I saw how easy it would be to fall prey to a disempowering discourse that would contribute to the victimization of sexual minorities from Southern[1] contexts or from marginalized groups within Northern contexts. In fact, an example of this discourse is readily apparent in Michèle's work with the World March of Women. In 1997, international delegates met to establish a platform of demands on a variety of issues. In order to avoid divisiveness on questions of sexual orientation, a "compromise" was accepted; this compromise allowed that demands based on sexual orientation be adopted on a country by country basis as opposed to being supported by all delegates.

In October 2001, this compromise was questioned by delegates meeting to discuss the progress of the March. They argued that this compromise is in fact discriminatory towards lesbians, and they called for an unconditional support of demands concerning sexual orientation on a worldwide level. A new vote on this question was quite divided:

[Haworth co-indexing entry note]: "Preface." Wehbi, Samantha. Co-published simultaneously in *Journal of Gay & Lesbian Social Services* (Harrington Park Press, an imprint of The Haworth Press, Inc.) Vol. 16, No. 1, 2004, pp. xxiii- xxviii; and: *Community Organizing Against Homophobia and Heterosexism: The World Through Rainbow-Colored Glasses* (ed: Samantha Wehbi) Harrington Park Press, an imprint of The Haworth Press, Inc., 2004, pp. xix- xxiv. Single or multiple copies of this article are available for a fee from The Haworth Document Delivery Service [1-800-HAWORTH, 9:00 a.m. - 5:00 p.m. (EST). E-mail address: docdelivery@haworthpress.com].

xix

delegates from Africa rejected the proposal en bloc with the support of delegates from Asia and the Middle East. The discussion was agitated, and the risk of a North-South split was quite perceptible. Some delegates from Southern countries expressed clearly homophobic remarks, while other delegates from Northern countries expressed remarks that can be seen as imperialist in nature, to the tune of "You don't understand, you're not there yet." These latter comments implied that in the North, we "have all understood" and that we are not confronted with homophobia within our feminist organizations!

A working subcommittee on this question, of which Michèle is a participant, has been charged with the task of developing a strategy and tools to assist in the process of adoption of demands related to sexual orientation. Members of the committee to date have been from Northern countries and have had difficulty grasping the issues that would arise for Southern women's groups should they support these demands in their own countries–Jitsuya, Sevilla and Goddard all refer to some of these issues. The arguments and proposed strategies sometimes betray a profound misunderstanding of cultural, political and economic realities, and often border on colonialist attitudes (e.g., "we Northerners need to educate Southerners about homophobia"). Moreover, the subcommittee has not yet deemed it necessary to work on this question with women, including activist lesbians, from the concerned world regions. Also necessary but not yet explored is an analysis of power relations and oppression between organizations and between feminists, including on dimensions of race and class.

In an increasingly globalizing world, as social service professionals of all stripes we are being called upon to forge international alliances on a variety of social issues (Rowe, Hanley, Repetur Moreno & Mould, 2000). Michèle's example demonstrates the dilemma that confronts us as we genuinely try to tackle homophobia and heterosexism within the context of North-South collaboration. At least two points deserve highlighting in this example. First, it is important not to homogenize Southern voices: power relations are present between North and South but also within Southern countries themselves. The women present at these meetings are not representative of the South but are members of groups that have the legitimacy and resources necessary to act as "representatives" of women in their country.

Second, there is a fine balance to be struck between recognizing that oppression exists against sexual minorities and not rendering them powerless in this very act of recognition. Resistance, in fact, is not the sole property of Northeners. Yet, centuries of colonialism and inequitable North-South relations have helped create a eurocentric vision within which respect for human rights is equated with the North, and "poor Southerners" are seen to suffer under the yoke of oppression. This conception is dangerous for at least two reasons. It creates a homogeneuous understanding of Northern contexts: as Meyer-Cook, Labelle and Nahas argue in this book, both historically and in present times, marginalized groups have existed within Northern contexts. And this narrow conception also hides the important history of resistance and continued struggles of these groups in Northern and Southern contexts. An important element of this struggle has been the fight against homophobia and heterosexism.

This collection presents five articles focusing on community organizing against homophobia and heterosexism in an effort to bring to light the history and contemporary face of resistence within Northern and Southern contexts. The articles are written by community organizers who have been active in resisting homophobia and heterosexism in their respective countries. In a certain sense, this book pays tribute to their courageous efforts, showing them not as helpless victims of oppression within their countries or marginalized communities, but as active agents of change in their own lives. Such a conception is essential for community organizers and other social service professionals to adopt in our collaborations to end homophobia and heterosexism. Although the articles differ in approach and context, they nonetheless bear several commonalities both in terms of theoretical foundation and in terms of several common themes to which I will later return in this preface.

Theoretically, the articles adopt an understanding of homophobia and heterosexism as forms of oppression that intersect with others such as racism and classism. There is no effort made on the part of the contributors to extract homophobia from racism or heterosexism from classism. On the contrary, the authors point to the complexity of oppression. Authors such as Hill Collins (1990) and Mullaly (1993) remind us that because our identities are formed of multiple elements, it follows that identity-based oppression can only be understood at the interesections of these elements–e.g., race, class, gender. As such, the authors in this collection are aware, for example, of how racism or sexism have helped define and shape the experience of homophobia and heterosexism in their countries.

A corollary argument is that identity-based oppression needs to be understood within its particular sociohistorical context[2] (Narayan, 1997; Young, 1990). For Meyer-Cook and Labelle, the legacy of racist colonial practices has contributed to the invisibility of Two-Spirited aboriginals within their own communities as well as within the broader Canadian context. Speaking of the Zimbabwean context, Goddard makes a similar reflection. In fact, he begins his discussion of the racist colonial legacies of homophobia and heterosexism that have contributed to a present-day situation where gays and lesbians defend their existence against current public discourse that sees it as a foreign intrusion.

Understanding oppression within its context and in its intersecting nature permits us as community organizers and other social service professionals involved in social change to develop more comprehensive solutions and responses to oppression. Underlying this understanding are echoes of the well-known epithet that there can be no true end to oppression as long as some are still oppressed. We may choose to start by addressing one manifestation of oppression in a strategic effort to simplify the task, but it is important that we conceive of this as one step in an ongoing process of fighting against oppression.

EMERGENT THEMES

Presented in this collection are articles from Peru, Hong Kong, Zimbabwe, Canada, and The Netherlands. In highlighting the complexity of oppression, the authors draw on several common themes: the importance of alliances; the importance of physical space; the tension with other communities of belonging; and transformation.

An intersectional understanding of oppression renders alliances essential, as problematical as they may be (Yuval-Davis, 1998). The articles highlight in varying degrees the necessity of building alliances with social service providers, the state, or community groups working to eradicate homophobia and heterosexism and/or other forms of oppression. These alliances are local, regional, and international in nature. While acknowledging the importance of these alliances, the authors point to the difficulties that can exist in forging equitable collaborations. This topic is the subject of the article by Jitsuya and Sevilla, who discuss their experiences in organizing GALF, a lesbian feminist group, in Peru in the early 1980s. Throughout their efforts to build important alliances with primarily heterosexual feminist groups and gay men's groups, it was necessary to find strategies to deal with the lesbophobia and sexism that GALF members encountered. Similarly, Nahas discusses the importance of alliances with social service providers and other gay and lesbian groups in organizing a Muslim gay and lesbian group in The Netherlands. In this case, alliances with international Muslim organizations were of the utmost importance in breaking the sense of isolation of Muslim gays and lesbians in the non-Muslim context of a European country and in the predominantly heterosexual context of Muslim communities. Alliances with the state and social service providers permitted the development of resources and a practice model useful in working with Muslim gays and lesbians.

As important as alliances is the presence of physical space. In his discussion of the emergence of the gay and lesbian liberation movement in Zimbabwe, Goddard highlights the importance of the first clubs in Harare that allowed sexual minorities to meet and to acknowledge each other's existence. Not only is the presence of physical space an important step towards challenging invisibility, it is also an important element for identity formation. For example, Jitsuya and Sevilla acknowledge the importance of the feminist coffee shop where many of the early founders of GALF had met and begun to develop their group and to shape their own identities as lesbians.

Another important theme is that of tension between members of sexual minority communities and their other communities of belonging. Bearing in mind an intersectional understanding of oppression, Meyer-Cook and Labelle discuss the homophobia and heterosexism that Two-Spirited peoples encounter on reservations or within their communities. Nahas alludes to a similar experience for Muslim gays and lesbians attempting to reconcile their religious belonging with their sexual orientation. Similarly, Jitsuya and Sevilla provide a detailed discussion of their encounters with lesbophobia within the feminist movement in Peru.

The final common theme is that of transformation. Each article bears witness to the transformation of individual efforts to deal with oppression into nascent movements able to mobilize many members as well as allies to respond to homophobia and heterosexism. As Carniol (2000) affirms, "social movements are able to translate an individual's desire for change into collective action" (p. 142). From the social get-togethers of early gay life in Harare to a burgeoning social movement able to defy a homophobic state, and from small-scale community actions to a large-scale legal campaign for *tongzhi* rights in Hong Kong, Goddard and To, respectively, offer powerful examples of this transformation.

Within this group process of transformation the seeds of broader social change are nourished, heralding the eventual eradication of homophobia, heterosexism and other forms of oppression. As social service professionals, we continue to be called upon to support this process of transformation in our research and practice. Our support can be, indeed must be, premised on a genuine appreciation of the empowered participation of sexual minorities worldwide in their own emancipation.

Samantha Wehbi
with the collaboration of Michèle Roy

NOTES

1. The terms North and South have been chosen to denote not so much geographical locations but historically rooted differential power relations between nations.
2. I have chosen to employ the term "sexual minorities" in recognition of the many context-specific terms that are used throughout the world and certainly by the authors in this collection. I am however aware that this term may not adequately reflect the notion of Two-Spiritedness. Nonetheless, the term "sexual minorities" is more inclusive than terms such as "gay" or "lesbian."

REFERENCES

Carniol, B. (2000). *Case critical: Challenging social work in Canada* (4th ed.). Toronto: Between the Lines.

Hill Collins, P. (1990). *Black feminist thought. Knowledge, consciousness, and the politics of empowerment*. London: Harper Collins Academic.

Mullaly, R. P (1993). *Structural social work: Ideology, theory, and practice*. Toronto: McClelland & Stewart.

Narayan, U. (1997). *Dislocating cultures: Identities, traditions, and Third World feminism*. New York: Routledge.

Rowe, W., Hanley, J., Repetur Moreno, E. & Mould, J. (2000). Voices of social work practice: International reflections on the effects of globalization. *Canadian Social Work*, 2 (1), 65-87.

Young, I. M. (1990). *Justice and the politics of difference*. Princeton, N.J.: Princeton University Press

Yuval-Davis, N. (1998). Beyond differences: Women, empowerment and coalition politics. In N. Charles & H. Hintjens (Eds.), *Gender, ethnicity and political ideologies* (pp. 168-189). New York: Routledge.

All the Bridges that We Build:
Lesbophobia and Sexism
Within the Women's and Gay Movements
in Peru

Nelly Jitsuya

Rebeca Sevilla

SUMMARY. This article traces the history of GALF, a Peruvian feminist lesbian group, illustrating its transformation from a consciousness raising group to a social change group organizing against lesbophobia and heterosexism. The authors rely on their experiences as two of the original co-founders of GALF to discuss the issues that have confronted the group's organizing efforts. The focus of the article is on the alliances that GALF has attempted to build both with the gay movement as well as with heterosexual feminist groups and services. The authors argue for the need to recognize the diversity of voices within feminist, gay, and lesbian groups, in an effort to build genuine alliances. *[Article copies available for a fee from The Haworth Document Delivery Service: 1-800-HAWORTH. E-mail address: <docdelivery@haworthpress.com> Website: <http://www.HaworthPress. com> © 2004 by The Haworth Press, Inc. All rights reserved.]*

KEYWORDS. Peru, GALF, lesbophobia, alliances, feminist, gay movement, community organizing

---

[Haworth co-indexing entry note]: "All the Bridges that We Build: Lesbophobia and Sexism Within the Women's and Gay Movements in Peru." Jitsuya, Nelly, and Rebeca Sevilla. Co-published simultaneously in *Journal of Gay & Lesbian Social Services* (Harrington Park Press, an imprint of The Haworth Press, Inc.) Vol. 16, No. 1, 2004, pp. 1-28; and: *Community Organizing Against Homophobia and Heterosexism: The World Through Rainbow-Colored Glasses* (ed: Samantha Wehbi) Harrington Park Press, an imprint of The Haworth Press, Inc., 2004, pp. 1-28. Single or multiple copies of this article are available for a fee from The Haworth Document Delivery Service [1-800-HAWORTH, 9:00 a.m. - 5:00 p.m. (EST). E-mail address: docdelivery@haworthpress.com].

Journal of Gay & Lesbian Social Services, Vol. 16(1) 2004
http://www.haworthpress.com/store/product.asp?sku=J041
© 2004 by The Haworth Press, Inc. All rights reserved.
10.1300/J041v16n01_01

Hay tantísimas fronteras
Que dividen a la gente,
Pero por cada frontera
Existe también un puente.[1]

(Valdés, cited in Anzaldúa, 1987, p. 85)

WE ARE EVERYWHERE!

There are lesbians and gays everywhere, including Peru. In every country the levels of democracy and fulfillment of human rights can also be measured by the treatment and living conditions of excluded social groups, such as gays and lesbians. Struggles against discrimination based on sexual orientation have adopted different strategies and forms of expression in each setting and culture.[2] As a result, the global and local awareness of lesbian and gay issues has increased in the last decades.

The first lesbian and gay organizing initiatives in Peru developed in parallel to democratic processes and were influenced by feminist movement proposals. The *Grupo de Autoconciencia de Lesbianas Feministas* (GALF) has been an important element in that process since the group's creation in 1983. GALF's need for a contextual, critical analysis and better understanding of its own processes is the major motivation underlying a research study on GALF's organizing process and development from the perspective of two protagonists, Nelly and Rebeca. This article is a preliminary review of some of the major organizing experiences and the political and social contexts within which they occurred.

The present article provides an overview of the interwoven relationships of GALF and the feminist and gay movements in the context of political and economic crises and transformations in Peru in the last few decades. Relying on GALF's experiences, the article attempts to understand the connections, tensions and dilemmas between lesbian identity and politics and to render visible the dynamics of sexism and lesbophobia. The article also attempts to identify successful strategies as well as obstacles in building links across differences, both within the group and in its relationships with others. The authors compare some aspects of GALF's processes with those of other groups in the Latin American and Caribbean region confronting issues of lesbian identity and lesbophobia.

In the 1970s the economic, social, political and cultural changes in Peru and in many Latin American and Caribbean countries were fertile grounds for structural transformations, women's political participation from basic demands to party politics, and the emergence of collective proposals and organizations led by women's organizations. Issues that were part of the daily lives of women, such as domestic violence, sexuality, power and women's positions in society were radically questioned. A call to see the private as political coupled with the demand for democracy in the nation as well as in the home were some of the proposals that characterized the emergence of an autonomous, pluralistic feminist movement that was respectful of differences.

However, the recognition, participation and inclusion of some groups' proposals like those of indigenous women, black women and lesbians found various degrees of resistance in the so called "progressive" parties, as well as in some alternative spaces like human rights and feminist organizations. Traditionally, human rights work has been focused on political activists who are harassed, murdered and reported missing during armed and social conflicts based on ideological convictions. Thus, domestic violence, discrimination based on sexual orientation or gender discrimination were not a priority. The gap between human rights agreements and commitments and their implementation and practices are still challenges for society as a whole, including for lesbian and gay organizations:

> the idea that there existed two feminisms began to take shape among intellectuals: one acceptable, which could be invited to take seat among forces of the left which attempted to reorganize the country; another, totally unacceptable, alien, the struggle of bourgeois lesbians against men. . . . (Golders cited in Alvarez, 1990, p. 98)

Lesbian feminists have participated in the construction of the movement since its birth. However, the presence of lesbians and the inclusion of lesbian issues on the agenda were not sufficiently recognized in those spaces, not only due to the sexual repression experienced at the time, but also because of the fear of losing "legitimacy," of being "accused" of being lesbians, or due to ignorance and prejudice. The Second Latin American and Caribbean Feminist *Encuentro*, held in Lima in 1983, illustrates this point. The subject of lesbianism was not on the agenda so lesbians called for a mini-workshop. The session began in a bar after dinner but drew so much interest that it reconvened in the plenary hall, where over half of the 600 participants present spent a very moving evening in what was perhaps the largest coming out event in the region (Bunch & Hinojosa, 2000). The first public lesbian response and challenge calling on (hetero) feminists to confront their lesbophobia had an impact on all participants, especially on lesbians. The "mini-workshop" at the *Encuentro* had a direct impact on the emergence of lesbian feminist groups organizing throughout Latin America from Chile and Peru to Brazil, Mexico, the Dominican Republic and many other countries, even several years later.

Given the various forms of discrimination that cross-cut all spheres, from the cultural to the legal; including all levels of external and internalized social repression, it is very difficult for lesbians to be visible. The lack of information, tolerance or respect towards different lifestyles, especially from the conservative Catholic Church and the traditional family structure have emerged as major obstacles to the right to live with dignity. Pioneer lesbian organizing efforts looked for alternatives to overcome isolation, to remedy the lack of information and to break away from sexual repression. The *Encuentros* provided the opportunity to meet other lesbians, exchange experiences and compare processes, both in the region, with some Latin American lesbians living outside the region and also with some foreigners from the US, Canada and Europe. The spirit and energy of the *Encuentros* gave many lesbians the final impulse to organize. Thus, in April 1984, the *Grupo de Autoconciencia de Lesbianas Feministas*–GALF (Lesbian Feminist Consciousness-Raising Group)–emerged as an autonomous group. GALF maintained a critical and constructive spirit in our work with the Feminist Movement and in the coordination of specific actions with other mixed gay and lesbian groups like the *Movimiento Homosexual de Lima*–MHOL–and *Acción para la Libreración Homosexual*–APLHO.

The few existing individual and collective initiatives began to multiply in Peru as well as in other parts of the Latin American region. Since 1987, the need to share our experiences and define regional strategies, led us to create a specific space for regional exchange, the Latin American and Caribbean Lesbian Feminist *Encuentros*. The first *Encuentro* was held in Cuernavaca, Mexico in 1987.

> Lesbian mothers, lesbian feminists, lesbian marxist leninists, lesbians working in gay movements, trade unions, lesbians non organized were meeting each other, sharing experiences, fighting, making love . . . and helping with the practical organization of the conference. The setting up of a Latin American Lesbian Network was a very important, but slow and difficult process. (Sevilla cited in Bunch & Hinojosa, 2000, p. 7)

The second lesbian *Encuentro* was to take place in Peru but due to the difficult economic and political situation in the country and divided internal opinions on this topic, it was held in Costa Rica in 1990. More lesbian feminist regional meetings took place in Costa Rica in 1990, Puerto Rico in 1993, Argentina in 1995 and Brazil in 1999.

Some international spaces provided by the International Lesbian Information Service (ILIS–founded in 1980), in its annual conferences, outreach and political actions such as during the Third United Nations World Conference on Women, held in Nairobi in 1985, and the regional lesbian workshops at the ILIS Conference held in Geneva in 1986, also affected lesbian international networking in Latin America and Asia. The International Lesbian and Gay Association (ILGA–founded in 1976) connected groups from the North and South, the South and South, and gays and lesbians from the same country. ILGA's efforts contributed to increasing solidarity, to the development of equal relationships among its members and to the development of organizations in countries where they did not exist.

From 1985 to 1991 GALF played an active role in rendering lesbian issues visible and in advocating for lesbian human rights in a diversity of contexts: from bars to sports teams, from activist organizations to public services, in closed circles and through the radio, to women and men, left to right, young and old, local and international. Our participation in regional and international forums was also a contributing factor to GALF's development and to the development of a Latin American and Caribbean lesbian network of activists.

The beginning of the 1990s in Peru was characterized by centralism, record inflation, political violence, the deterioration of institutions that guarantee democracy, a parallel government structure; increasing mass media manipulation; pressure and threats to social and political forces opposed to the dominant regime, increase of migration, among many other social changes. GALF's existence was severely affected by these external factors: an important number of members migrated temporarily; time limitations for voluntary work for those who stayed became more pressing; the fragmentation of organizations and the increasing atmosphere of fear also limited GALF's organizing potentials. In addition, GALF had begun from "scratch," so the lack of "know-how" to manage its rapidly-growing attendance to the Monday night meetings, from eight to almost 40 lesbians every week, the weak infrastructure and insufficient human resources to respond to a variety of needs and problems and expectations from a very diverse group of lesbians had an impact on GALF's internal dynamics. GALF implemented a range of "informal" services and activities: consciousness raising sessions, coun-seling, conflict resolution interventions, sports, cultural events, as well as the publication and distribution of a lesbian newsletter called *Al Margen*. In addition, GALF members participated in workshops, panel discus-sions, and radio interviews.

Some GALF members also eventually wore more than one "hat" given their activism and work in more structured and professional nongovernmental social service organizations like women's centers. Other members were also involved in the only legally recognized and mainly male organization, *Movimiento Homosexual de Lima*-MHOL. All this exhausting grassroots work, pressure and lack of continuity led to GALF's temporary dissolution.

The political and economic backlashes and the emergency of the AIDS crisis affected gay and lesbian organizing dynamics, provoking an increase in homophobia but also of solidarity among minority groups. The new context called for greater joint efforts and for challeng-ing dominant patterns related to diversity, such as questioning the social positions of gay men and lesbians in society and within their own groups. Another challenge was the need for inclusion of bisexuals, transgendered individuals, people living with HIV, sex workers, and others and in finding points of convergence in the different ways of fac-ing discrimination. These developments affected GALF members to various degrees. Even to this date, there are still some tensions around priorities, perspectives and processes in coalition work.

In 1996, a reorganized GALF came back to the local political scene characterized by the demand for democratic changes. GALF members re-initiated the organization of workshops for lesbians, as well of vari-ous activities of the women's and the gay and lesbian movements in Lima. The local and international scene and actors had changed, as well as the ways to do activism: lesbianism became more visible, but dis-crimination persists in many ways. The legal and social position of les-bians and gays had improved in many parts of the world. In Latin America, there were lesbian groups in almost every country. Despite of-ten repressive and hostile local environments, positive legal changes have been achieved in some countries. However, lesbian organizing ef-forts and exchanges continue to face new challenges:

> the *encuentros* became the space for meaningful and sometimes polarized debates, as the movement grew, diversified, and faced new challenges, such as the severe impact of structural adjustment policies and increasing violence in the region. Some of the critical

questions raised at the *encuentros* included the meaning of political autonomy and the need to make alliances with other social movements, dealing with ideological diversity within the movement, problems of organizational structure, leadership, representation and the role of lesbian visibility within the women's movement. (Bunch & Hinojosa, 2000, p. 10)

Contexts have changed, and so have GALF members. We have more experience, and less fear; we have new diverse approaches, priorities, skills, living and working styles, etc. We have learned more about lesbianism through experiences ranging from the intimacy of daily living to academic gay and lesbian studies, from local and long-distance relationships to working in grassroots women's group and in global networks and initiatives. We have developed more contacts and networks, not only with other lesbians, but also with other movements and organizations advocating for human rights locally and globally.

GALF initiated a process to revise our objectives which are: to sensitize public opinion and advocate for the human rights and full citizenship of lesbians; to strengthen our internal organization; and to exchange experiences with other organizations. Communication technologies have challenged and positively affected GALF's participation process in all stages, including the membership living abroad.

Local dynamics generated by several processes have been useful in exposing the fundamental aspects of a common spirit, visions and methodologies. These processes included: the general GALF assembly convened in December 2000, the development of a lesbian supplement *Labia* to the mainly male gay magazine *Paradero*, our participation in the preparatory process towards the United Nation World Conference Against Racism, held in South Africa in September 2001, and the parallel Non Governmental Forum. These processes are not smooth, since economic, political and social challenges *place* organizations like GALF in a critical position. Some of our weaknesses and the obstacles to fulfilling our visions have also become evident, as well as our need for a strategic plan and basic facilities that may provide greater continuity to our current plans.

ORIGINS: WE ARE FAMILY!

In March 1984, we began to feel restless as a result of events like the "mini" workshop on lesbianism and patriarchy during the Third Latin

American and Caribbean Feminist *Encuentro*, the course given by Charlotte Bunch on Feminist Theory and Strategies for the Women's Movement. We also began to feel the time was ripe to begin discussing an issue that was vital to us but was silenced or openly criticized by the majority in all the spheres in which we moved. Three women (Silvia Parramón, Nelly Jitsuya and a third woman) convened a meeting to find out if there was interest in organizing as lesbians. Twelve women answered this first call and laid the groundwork for what was to be the first lesbian feminist group in Peru.

The first discussions had to do with what term or label would be used to describe ourselves. Every word that was brought had negative connotations in popular usage. The group decided to use the word "lesbian" anyway and imbue it with positive contents from their personal experiences of fulfillment in loving other women. The initial identification as "lesbians" was central in the early stages of organizing. At the time nobody questioned or criticized the validity of organizing around a "lesbian identity," even as we recognized that it was a social and historical construct. It was strategically useful to do so at that stage: to name the unnamed was an affront to the double moral standard and hypocrisy in Lima. It also exposed the exclusion, invisibility and intolerance women had experienced in our own lives, within our biological family, before the law, in our jobs and other social contexts. Our lesbianism created a sense of commonality, what others have referred to as "sisterhood" and we called "family," that justified organizing separately under this category. These experiences created and strengthened our group identity and cohesion. However, group identity did not ensure the survival of the group, on the contrary, it had the effect of not taking adequate consideration of differences amongst us. In retrospect, we may argue that a unitary, cohesive group identity can be the main obstacle to long-term group survival, as it does not account for and respond to the multiple and diverse visions and needs of lesbians.

In organizing around the general banner of lesbian feminism, we initially gave less priority to the many aspects in which we were, in fact, different: in terms of class, ethnic origin, education, age, occupation, and also in organizing abilities, visibility, power dynamics, ways to stand for our rights, etc. There was a more urgent need to find the common ground before looking at our differences. Looking from the distance, since we were the only lesbian feminist group in Peru, there were many (un)realistic expectations and many hidden (and sometimes wrong) assumptions; for instance, that we were all the same or that the meaning of our ideological definition as "lesbian feminist" would be understood by every GALF member in the same way.

Exclusion and invisibility are common threads of lesbian experience in the Latin American and Caribbean (LAC) region and, indeed, the world. As Csömyei and Palumbo, from Argentina, point out, ". . . to be a lesbian means, for many of us, to be condemned to silence, self-marginalization and, solitude" (Csömyei & Palumbo, 1996, p. 153). Likewise, the Latin American and Caribbean lesbian workshop at the 8th ILIS Conference, held in Geneva in March 1986, concluded that, ". . . lesbians of these countries share common experiences; the majority of them are isolated and invisible; it is difficult for them to be independent and therefore they are extremely vulnerable to repression . . . " (Irving, 1987, p. 12).

The next logical step, after recognizing that this identification as lesbians was of vital strategic importance, was to find out more about what that meant in our lives and how it affected other aspects of our being. We also attempted to understand the origins of such virulent reactions to our existence, often to the point of denying that we existed at all. We wanted to create a space where we could explore these issues in depth, as existing spaces–lesbian bars, women's groups, gay groups–were too limiting.

Again, this process was not unique to us. Various lesbian and lesbian-feminist groups that were formed afterwards in the LAC region share a similar experience. Women from the Argentinean group *Las Lunas y las Otras* write:

> We got together spontaneously because of the need to create a space in which we could tell our own stories, where we could strengthen ourselves against daily discrimination, and where getting to know the others could enlighten our own self-knowledge. (Csömyei & Palumbo, 1996, p. 156)

In these intentional, relatively protected spaces we at last had the opportunity to try out alternative interpretations to our experiences of lesbianism and lesbophobia and to establish and strengthen a connection to a group with whom we felt we shared common experiences and a common sexual identity. Indeed, as Viñuales (1999) argues:

> The perception of isolation and the need to construct a history or narration (*subculturization*), of finding 'points of reference' or ideological and emotional support with which to face the stigma,

lead individuals to get in touch with a new social world formed by similar others. . . . The contact with similar others not only legitimates what one *is*, but also produces a reification of the 'lesbian' fact which, in re-writing past history of female homosexuality (Safo of Lesbos), ends up explaining and constructing one's own present identity. (pp. 57-58)

From March to September of 1984 our small group met on a weekly basis in closed sessions. We adopted the name *Grupo de Autoconciencia de Lesbianas Feministas*–GALF (Lesbian Feminist Consciousness-Raising Group) as we defined that our initial objective would be to engage in a process of questioning and transforming past interpretations regarding lesbianism and constructing new, positive images of ourselves as lesbians and as women.

We were an enthusiastic bunch, with little literature at our disposal, no previous experience or intensive courses about sexuality and even less experience in consciousness-raising groups, except for training courses in left parties on the part of some. Most of the literature came from the United States and Europe, and little of it was translated. But perhaps all this added to our curiosity and to the excitement of learning together, and of entering unknown territories. Humor and creativity were always present, maybe as a way to relax tensions, deal with aggressions, fulfill our needs or as survival mechanisms. GALF was a heterogeneous and colorful group of local and foreign women, and women of indigenous, African, Asian or Caucasian descent; our ages ranged from early 20s to early 40s; our educational levels, from no college education to graduate degrees; our housing situation, from homeless to living in a wealthy area of town; very few were living independently. Only a few had experiences living abroad, others had hardly left the capital or only knew their parents' place of origin. One was a single mother since 1983 and another decided to become one in 1990. However, it is interesting to note that while we recognized and acknowledged the diversity among us from the very beginning, and even took pride in being such a heterogeneous group, we did little to explore how those differences affected our lives. On the other hand, we shared some level of organizing experience in the feminist movement and/or left political parties. And we all identified as lesbians and as feminists, with varying degrees of conviction.

Each weekly session lasted from three to five hours. They were not recorded and no notes were taken and kept. Knowing that we would be dealing with sensitive personal issues, special care was put in creating a safe and respectful atmosphere and some basic characteristics of participation were laid down: continuous attendance; commitment to stay for the entire session; each person would have the opportunity to speak about each topic without interruption; no new participant would be admitted once the process had been initiated; the choice of location had to prioritize privacy and absence of distracting elements; and commitment to confidentiality regarding what was shared in the sessions. Although the issue of alcohol consumption during sessions was never brought up, they happened to be alcohol-free. Several of us did smoke a lot and no one complained.

> Each meeting was a feast and a respite we gave ourselves in the face of social pressure; hours flew by, specially [sic] in the consciousness-raising sessions. . . . We also used these meetings to tell each other the latest gossip, to fall in love, how to handle our first relationship and sexual experience and fantasies. . . . Our meetings were charged with emotions and, often, also with tensions; but joy, as well as a sense of humor, predominated. We went from tragedy to amusement and from laughter to crying with incredible ease. (GALF, 1997, p. 8)

The issues we covered were also diverse: Coming out or the process of informing others about our sexual and affectionate preferences, why or why not tell somebody and when, what influenced our orientation or choice; invisibility, assuming roles, attitudes towards roles; couple relationships; flirting; breaking up; motherhood; socioeconomic, age, and other differences. The process that unfolded closely resembled the stages described by Pam Allen, who described the process that unfolded in her small group in San Francisco in four stages: opening up, sharing, analyzing and abstracting (Bunch, 1987).

The first stage described by Allen, opening up, was essential in establishing the foundations for GALF's initial work. It was at this point, our first meetings, that we identified common interests and decided on the general orientation or aims of the group. In the second stage, sharing, the factor that played a key role was the construction of trust and mutual support. This resulted in greater group cohesion, the development of a common language, as well as personal and group empowerment. It was a process of re-inventing ourselves, of transforming the narrow and negative stereotypes and myths used against lesbians and imbuing them with our own interpretations thereby broadening the spectrum of possibilities. The other two stages unfolded in a second period of GALF's development, as we moved out from the closed group and immediate necessities and began to publish a newsletter, *Al Margen.*

FROM PERSONAL/GROUP EMPOWERMENT
TO POLITICAL ACTION

The safe haven of a closed consciousness-raising group provided the necessary setting to voice and validate our differing experiences as lesbians and as women in our diverse contexts. It made us take pride in our strengths and in the subversiveness underlying our resistance to heteropatriarchy. It made us strengthen our trust in ourselves and in each other as a group. We had transformed our divergence from the socially sanctioned norm from shame to pride: As Minh-ha notes, "Otherness becomes empowerment, critical difference when it is not given but recreated" (Minh-ha, 1988, p. 75).

However, this process, which had been going on for six months was then interrupted by two major events. First, the women's coffee shop *La otra cara de la luna*–the first (and only) feminist women-only cultural space, in which four of us worked and where all of us often met–was forced to close down due to financial problems. Second, conflictive couple relationships led to some couples temporarily withdrawing from the sessions.

After a brief period of recovery from these upsetting circumstances, the group met again to review its progress and to re-define its perspectives for the future. The group agreed to bring closure to this "preparatory" consciousness-raising period and to tackle some of our other original objectives. We wanted to find ways to share with others the results of our discoveries about internal dynamics, to promote the creation of similar groups and to broaden membership in ours, to influence public opinion through articles in local media, and to propose the inclusion of lesbian issues in the other groups and organizations we belonged to.

We made the decision to start producing a monthly newsletter *Al Margen*, as our first strategic activity. And we identified other feminists as our "natural" allies–we felt that as part of the local feminist movement, the rest of the movement had no choice but to incorporate and defend our specific demands as lesbians.

ARE "NATURAL" ALLIANCES PERFECT?

During our consciousness-raising period, the feminist movement in Lima had been holding open evaluation meetings in order to set up a better structure. We had been participating on an individual basis or as members of the women's coffee shop collective. During one of our sessions, the question was put forth as to whether or not we should make GALF formally visible in this space. There was a week-long and passionate discussion as to the advantages and disadvantages of visibility versus remaining anonymous. Though many women in the feminist movement knew that we were lesbians, we had never discussed lesbian issues extensively, either at a personal level or in groups. However, we all agreed that this was a necessary next step if we wanted to confront lesbophobia in our lives and to change the situations of exclusion and discrimination against lesbians. As GALF members we considered that an autonomous, pluralistic feminist movement, of which we were a part, and that was respectful of differences also needed to confront existing barriers related to sexual politics and homophobia.

We planned our first public presentation by agreeing to attend a feminist movement meeting, and provide real faces and names to the "invisible" topic called lesbianism. For some of the women present it was maybe the first time they saw "a real lesbian." We had a vague idea of the long-term implications and consequences our presentation.

Our self-identification as lesbians went hand in hand with an awareness of lesbophobia. To the well-known slogan "Lesbians are everywhere," we could add: so is lesbophobia. As we had suspected, the initial reaction to our presentation was not of open acceptance, but neither was it of open rejection. There was a protracted silence followed by an intervention on a totally different subject. Finally, one of the most respected leaders of the movement at the time, welcomed us, expressed her admiration for our courage and concluded that she was afraid that the movement might not yet be ready for us. But who in the movement, when and how they would be ready was not clear either. Perhaps, they would have been happier if we had continued working only on other movement issues as we had done until then.

On the other hand, we were not asking to be part of the feminist movement. We felt that as women and as lesbians, we had been a vital part of the movement for years. The shift was that now we were demanding that the movement openly and explicitly recognize our existence as lesbians, as well as our contributions to the movement, and that lesbian issues be part of the agenda, including the implications of compulsory heterosexuality for women in general, challenging from a radical perspective male domination and the traditional division of power between sexes. Thus, we continued our work in the Reproductive Rights Commission, as well as in drafting the declaration of women's basic rights presented by the Women's Rights Commission to presidential candidates.[3] We continued participating and co-organizing campaigns around the End Violence Against Women Day, International Women's Day, and other movement initiatives.

At the same time, two GALF members (Silvia Parramón and Nelly Jitsuya) carried out interviews with the three main Peruvian feminist publications and one documentation center on their policies regarding the inclusion of lesbian issues: Gina Vargas for the magazine *Viva*, Susana Galdos for the bulletin *Manuela*, Rosa Dominga Trapasso for the documentation center *Creatividad y Cambio*, and Armida Testino for the magazine *La Tortuga*. Summaries of these interviews were published in the first two issues of GALF's bulletin *Al Margen*–April and June, 1985. The four interviewees agreed that lesbianism was a valid sexual orientation. Their responses also revealed views ranging from blatant contradictions and prejudices, for instance, that lesbianism is a middle class phenomenon, to an understanding that this was a critical issue for the feminist movement as a whole. None of the publications had included lesbian issues until then, although all of them had considered the possibility.

In an internal GALF evaluation meeting two years later in 1987, the publication of these interviews and the confrontational attitude of the interviewers themselves were viewed as the main sources of uneasiness and unexpressed tensions between GALF and other feminists, and the potential source of a lesbian-straight divide in the movement. Some feminists disagreed with the portrait of feminist publications raised by GALF in *Al Margen*. For others, GALF members were overreacting to the responses of the interviewees and were assuming a position of victims. Others were indifferent. Regardless of the differences in reaction, the article made visible unstated and informal magazine policies and helped feminist groups to confront the fact that these policies had to change: lesbians and lesbian issues were indeed totally absent from the main feminist publications. The emergence of more visible lesbians and lesbian topics provoked some uneasiness and tensions, and highlighted the difficulties of adjusting to local lesbian activism.

However, it is questionable if there ever was a lesbian-straight divide in the Peruvian feminist movement. Throughout this period, GALF members did not break the communication chain unilaterally. We continued working shoulder to shoulder; we took our space participating in meetings or commissions, we spoke openly about implications of various issues for lesbians. In fact, GALF developed gradually closer relationships with several straight feminists working in different women's centers. Sometimes the relationship went beyond activism, as we invited them to join us in lesbian bars, discos or parties. As a result, some were more "ready" than others to work with us, respect our work and ways of working. In general, many of them were very helpful in contributing to GALF's activities, providing access to their center's facilities: meeting rooms, use of typewriters, telephones, providing paper and staying with us long hours mimeographing copies of *Al Margen*. Women's organizations supported GALF's work in many ways. GALF held its weekly meetings at *Centro de la Mujer Peruana Flora Tristan, Movimiento Manuela Ramos* and *Asociación Aurora Vivar*. In short,

> I think there has been an opening, but I would call it an intellectual opening. In practice it is often contradicted. For instance, there is very little coverage of issues of concern to lesbians in feminist periodicals. And on the other hand, there is still a great fear of the word 'lesbian'; even feminists fear it because they still fear being labeled a bunch of lesbians. (Jitsuya cited in Lorenzo, 1985, p. 33)

However, through the years, we became aware of how conflicts between lesbian and straight feminists were affecting groups in other countries of the region. Among the most disturbing was the conflict that arose in neighboring Chile with the publication of an interview with three members of the lesbian feminist collective *Ayuquelén*. In the interview, they mentioned the women's center *La Morada* as the place where they held meetings. In response, *La Morada* wrote a letter to the editor claiming that the interview was "superficial and sensationalist" and that the interviewees themselves were contributing to reinforcing "existing prejudice, harming the rights of individuals" (Colectivo Coordinador de la Casa de la Mujer "La Morada," 1987). But the key to their outrage lay in the fact that the interviewees had mentioned their institution, at a time when homosexuality was criminalized by the Chilean Constitution of the Pinochet regime:

> if [Ayuquelén] wanted to 'visibilize' their own reality, but remaining anonymous due to fear of possible backlash from a society as repressive as ours, they should have taken into consideration that the same backlash could be directed against organizations such as 'La Morada,' that works publicly on behalf of all women for a more just society. (Colectivo Coordinador de la Casa de la Mujer "La Morada," 1987, p. 63)

This was a hard blow for Ayuquelén, since they did not have their own space and depended on La Morada to hold their meetings. We may also note that they were receiving anonymous death threats in their post office box.

The fear of many straight feminists and feminist organizations of being mistaken for lesbians or advocates of lesbian issues is understandable, not justifiable. This identification of feminism with lesbianism had been long suggested, promoted and used by sensationalist media as a way of ridiculing and attacking the feminist movement or individual prominent women. Many feminists did not feel comfortable in our presence, or were afraid to deal with us and with lesbian issues because of several known and unknown reasons:

> Whether due to fear of being 'mistaken for lesbians,' or because the priorities under consideration were other than lesbian, heterosexual Argentinean feminists did not usually see the presence of lesbians within the feminist movement as positive. However, and despite the fact that they were deliberately excluded, many lesbian activists feel ourselves to be feminists, though not all declare it explicitly. (Csömyei & Palumbo, 1996, p. 155)

Likewise, one of the conclusions of the Latin American and Caribbean lesbian workshop at the 8th International Lesbian Information Service Conference in Geneva, March 1986, was that:

> the majority of heterofeminists are intolerant of lesbianism and because of socioeconomic realities within their countries their struggle is almost always directed towards other sectors (issues)–lesbian struggles are not seen as a priority. (Irving, 1987, p. 12)

The homophobia, resistance, obstacles, open rejection and exclusion expressed by many heterosexual feminists towards lesbians in the region led many lesbians to organize separately. This is clearly noted by lesbian feminists organizing in Mexico, Chile and Costa Rica:

> In Mexico City there has always been a lack of lesbian space within the hetero-feminist community, even though a large percentage of the feminist community is lesbian! Of course, these women don't identify as being 'lesbian' but 'as being in love with women.' (Pérez in Irving, 1987, p. 12)

The women who began [*Ayuquelén* in Chile] had originally belonged to various feminist groups, but they had grown tired of experiencing yet further discrimination: despite the common discourse between Lesbian and heterosexual feminist about gender oppression, the political urgency of the social mobilization to overthrow the dictatorship did not allow for a deeper analysis of different sexual options. (Rivera, 1996, p. 143)

The dearth of information on lesbian feminism in [Costa Rica], combined with the lack of feminist consciousness of the majority of lesbians and the latent fear of rejection by feminist groups, the women's movement and by society in general, created permanent obstacles to our project. (Madden, 1996, p. 130)

The lesbian-straight divide experienced by many lesbian groups in the region during this period had profound effects in organizational processes and led to greater questioning and dilemmas on all sides. We had to know why loving other women sexually, as well as in other senses, caused so much discomfort and rejection. We needed to know and share the knowledge regarding what lay at the roots of lesbophobia in the feminist movement, as well as in some lesbian circles.

Just as the generic term "humankind" rendered women invisible, so the general term "women" rendered our diversity as women invisible–much as the generic term "homosexual" renders lesbians invisible). Thus, a politics based on a common identity or a universal subject (women, homosexuals, or even lesbians), whether identity was understood as an essential given or as a social construct, has often led to the oppression or marginalization of those others who are not included explicitly under that identity. Difference thus becomes the grounds for discord, as well as for re-thinking identity-based politics.

In the case of the feminist movement, in the early years, it was obvious that the discourse on women did not include explicitly enough our sexual diversity nor other aspects of our experiences in which we were different from each other. GALF looked for more explicit inclusion in feminist political proposals and in services offered by feminist organizations. Some feminist groups were more open to change than others and included sexual orientation and lesbian issues in their sexuality courses, public presentations and debates. But the word "woman" referred almost exclusively to heterosexual women in most studies, practices and services.

ON COMMITMENTS, ALLIANCES
AND RESPONSIBILITIES WITH THE GAY MOVEMENT

If at the local level, our "natural" allies, other feminists, were not aware that they were overlooking lesbians, women of African descent, etc., in their agendas, what could we expect from our colleagues in MHOL? Its founders–poets, artists, professionals, students and employees of various social strata–believed that lesbians would perceive themselves as included in the use of the word "homosexual." This process was in no way unique. The International Gay Association (IGA), founded in Coventry, England in 1978, changed its name many years later in 1986 to include lesbians. In the Latin American region, the *Encontros Hommosexuais do Brasil* (Brazilian Homosexual Meetings), similarly decided to change its name many years later in its 7th Meeting in 1993.

Labels aside, GALF accepted invitations to participate in MHOL's meetings and coordinated joint actions. On some occasions, alliances were dictated by external circumstances, as was the case of our joint participation in the 7th Conference of the International Gay Association (Toronto, 1985). Due to IGA's affirmative action policy, the Conference organizers offered MHOL two travel grants under the condition that a woman be included. They, therefore, offered GALF one of the grants.

In 1988 MHOL faced an internal crisis between two forces: a group of conservative and closeted gay men versus a more democratic, open and diverse group. Eventually, both sub-groups agreed to choose a lesbian, Rebeca Sevilla–also a member of GALF–as the organization's Director for the first time in its history. This decision carried some changes. MHOL became a more mixed and open human rights organization. Its internal structure, organizational culture, budget allocation, services, political and cultural strategies changed. It had the advantage of being the only legally-recognized gay and lesbian organization in Peru to receive funding from an international cooperation agency. Its response to the AIDS crisis opened new spaces to speak about sexuality, different Peruvian lifestyles, to organize publicly, and to cooperate with local or national governments in AIDS prevention campaigns. MHOL also maintained an active participation on human rights and anti-discrimination forums at the local and international levels and made its services widely available.

GALF and MHOL experienced the initial euphoria, intense working days, the ups and downs of the search for spaces for our internal dynamics, as well as the burnout and the limits of operating as grassroots organizations. We were different from each other in terms of visions, approaches, work methodologies, and institutional and individual protagonism. Gender discrimination became manifest in the lack of interest on the part of several MHOL members when a woman spoke, and in the resistance to take women's experiences or perspectives seriously. Power differences were also expressed in the roles assigned: who leads, participates in international events, does the "clean" or the "dirty" jobs. There appeared to be a hidden, unilateral or mutual, competition at the internal level or with other organizations to demonstrate which group had greater political power. But there's no evil that can last for a hundred years and there's no lesbian who could stand it. It took some time for some gay men to understand or begin to realize, within their limitations, the connection between sexism and heterosexism. A review of the magazine *Conducta (Im)propia* published by MHOL illustrates the gradual inclusion of women in this process: the inclusion of images of women, the use of nonsexist language and the participation of lesbians in the decision-making of the editorial committee.

At the beginning of the 1990s, our demands for inclusion and visibility of lesbian rights in the agenda began to be incorporated. However, the informal organization and structuring of our work, together with our decision not to seek foreign financial aid began to show their limitations. The various attempts at reorganizing GALF (day-long sessions on lesbian organizing and conflict resolution, workshops on confronting fears, informal consultation meetings, etc.) did not lead to consistent results. We organized around commissions with greater autonomy. The lesbian studies group received small grants for its work but did not manage to publish the results of its work. It seemed easier to work against something or somebody rather than formulate proactive proposals. In time, some of our differences within GALF became more visible: differences between those with political and those with social interests, between members and users of GALF's services, between GALF members and GALF-MHOL members, between feminists and nonfeminists, between those who performed intellectual and political roles and those who were engaged in manual/practical roles. Another important difference was that of the levels of experience between members.

The inclusion and participation of lesbians in MHOL, especially of GALF members–because of their visions, perspectives and accumulated experiences–had a marked influence on MHOL's services. Also influential was the advice provided by institutions such as AIDSCOM–the primary US AID-funded AIDS communication support program–on research interventions, special training and educational material for target audiences. Advice from such institutions combined with the active participation of lesbians had a great influence on the implementation, evaluation and follow-up of over a dozen services provided by MHOL: AIDS hot line, peer education program, safe sex, documentation center, sports, counseling, legal advice, debates, video presentations, parties, consciousness-raising groups for lesbian, gay and mixed audiences, to name a few.

The participation of GALF members in MHOL was the decision of individual members as an attempt to contribute to changing a *supposedly* gender-mixed organization into an organization that was *in fact* mixed. However, this decision generated differences and tensions among lesbians, both within and outside GALF. The institutionalization of a gender perspective in MHOL's institutional policies in the 1990s, brought improvements in terms of women's participation. However, it did not always include concrete mechanisms to evaluate and ensure continuity in the medium and long terms. The presence of lesbians did not guarantee by itself the analysis, the generation of proposals and the understanding of a gender perspective. As a result, some of the positive discrimination measures to promote the participation of lesbians were partially implemented or not at all.

Close to the end of the honeymoon period (1988-1992) of lesbian involvement in MHOL, gaps began to be felt. Some technical skills in the provision of services were strengthened, but they did not necessarily go hand in hand with the capacities to sustain a more plural, flexible and diverse organization that could achieve a balanced response to what was urgent, what was possible and what was realistic.

> Although in the course of time, there has been a greater acknowledgment of lesbian participation, this has become insufficient due to the lack of continuity, of mechanisms to monitor the implementation of agreements. But to be a lesbian or gay or a member of any sexual minority as part of a social movement is not enough if our efforts are not related to our capacity to support and develop broader perspectives, as well as participatory dynamics and experiences, trying to achieve a balance between the internal organization and its external social context. Let's link human rights with sexual rights, democracy and citizenship rights. (Sevilla, 2000)

CHANGES BEGIN AT HOME:
OUR LOCAL STONEWALL

Within GALF we had the strong conviction that we could not stand alone if we wanted to have some sort of political influence in changing the situations of exclusion and discrimination in which we found ourselves as lesbians. We also believed that a feminist vision would not be complete if it failed to question and eradicate lesbophobia and heterosexism. As Bunch suggests, "We, as lesbians, are a minority. We cannot survive alone. We will not survive alone, but if we do not survive the entire women's movement will be defeated and female oppression will be reenacted in other forms" (Bunch, 1987, p. 180). We should observe at this point, that although lesbians may be a minority in terms of the population in general, this situation may be questioned in terms of participation in the feminist movement in Lima. Unlike Bunch's experience of lesbians being a minority in the women's movement, when we looked around us as we organized various feminist movement activities, we often saw that much of the driving force for those activities came from lesbians. Likewise, at the peak of GALF's enrollment, our numbers were equal to or exceeded that of the women working at the NGO that offered us a space for our meetings. However, more important than relative numbers and group positioning was the quality of radical lesbian proposals raised by GALF: question compulsory heterosexuality, demand control over our own bodies and open,

> a space, until then unexplored, from which to question fundamental aspect of the lives of human beings: their sexuality. To the extent that sexuality is the object of authoritarianism, repression and silence, distorting and condemning, to open the possibility of facing it openly contributes to promote more democratic relationships and visions, as well as to generate a climate of respect for differences. (Vargas, 1993, p. 2)

Through our closest feminist (formerly) heterosexual friends, we were able to understand in greater depth the discomfort and fear we saw in some of our fellow activists in the feminist movement. This led us to think of strategies to change those beliefs, expressions and assumptions. We had brainstorming sessions, long discussions until we decided to organize a workshop on lesbianism with the aim of confronting lesbophobia in the feminist movement. We sent personal invitations to thirty feminist leaders, all of whom attended the session. We later found out why: Many were surprised that they had been invited and went to find out why; others felt that if they did not go, they would be considered lesbophobic. The impact was also felt among those women who were not invited: Why was I not included? Do they think I'm lesbophobic?

The workshop, which took place in 1986, was a success due to the turnout and because we achieved its main aims: to build real communication bridges, to begin the process of demystification of lesbian existence, to strengthen our connections and to create an atmosphere of camaraderie. Above all, it became clear that the challenge ahead pertained to all of us: To reflect our discourse on inclusion in our actions. Vargas (1993) discusses the impact of this workshop that engaged participants in imaginary games:

> I remember that once they made us participate in an imaginary demonstration in the San Martin Square, where movement posters intermingled but didn't get mixed up, each one in its slot: lesbians with their posters on free sexual choice and heterosexual women with their posters on violence, hunger, discrimination at work, etc. . . . But at a certain point in the imaginary game, posters got mixed up in a confusing movement and identities got mixed up. And then, several of us ended up with posters that said "I'm a lesbian . . ." and were paralyzed just imagining a situation of such proportions. We all recognized later that we had wanted to let go of the poster and run away, in case someone saw us, that the press would notice us, that television cameras would surprise us. (p. 5)

The struggle against lesbophobia in the feminist movement in Lima also benefited greatly from the various opportunities to work together in discussion groups and in organizing campaigns and celebrations. GALF members were part of the movement's new structure, *Colectivo Coordinador Feminista* (the Feminist Coordinating Collective). We were constantly present in various movement activities, forging alliances and friendships, earning respect for our commitment to common causes. On the other hand, lesbian issues were explicitly addressed in International Women's Day celebrations and Non-Violence Against Women campaigns, as well as in other movement initiatives. A turning point for the feminist movement occurred in June, 1986. The *Colectivo Coordinador Feminista* issued a public statement to the mass media demanding an end to arbitrary police harassment of lesbians.

> I remember the disco in Huaraz Street, in Breña. We used to go there in large groups to drink beer and dance. One Saturday, when we weren't there, the police raided the premises; channel 2, one of the national television channels, filmed the raid and our friends and acquaintances appeared in the screen as common offenders, captured by the camera when they were being led out with shoves from the premises to buses and police cars, many of them unsuccessfully trying to cover their faces. We protested, we talked with congress members, but the video was broadcasted (sic) once and again; several women lost their jobs and several others their families and friends. (Vargas, 1993, p. 6)

Around seventy women were taken to the police station for individual questioning, receiving abusive physical treatment and verbal abuse ("we'll teach you to be women") from the police. They were finally released during curfew hours, putting their personal safety at risk.[4] The TV report was released as a prime-time news three times in a week at peak rating hours. None of the victims wanted to denounce the abuse by the police and the TV channel.

However, this negative experience also brought some positive developments. The feminist movement publicly expressed its solidarity, demanding sanctions for the police officers responsible for the raid and abuse, and demanding an antidiscrimination law to protect individuals from all forms of discrimination based on their sexual orientation. For GALF, this incident reaffirmed our conviction and persistence in working on these issues. The urgency to come out publicly as lesbians, with the support of others, became clearer than ever.

NEW DIRECTIONS AND DILEMMAS

We are part of the emergence of a new movement of lesbians and gays, composed of organizations and initiatives with various creative forms of formal and informal organization. These emerged as responses to various needs and to the desire to transform existing realities. We broadened the spaces for social participation and the social agenda, traditionally inaccessible to lesbians and gays. We contributed to the promotion of information and knowledge regarding our rights, our bodies, sexualities and lifestyles, leading to a broadening of awareness, self-confidence and the ability to exercise power.

In this process of reflection on our lives, beliefs, values, and motivations, we began to grow, even if this growth was not at the same rate and with the same intensity for each one of us. On one hand, we realized that this empowering process could be repeated with other groups of lesbians, and the internal group dynamic was a good space to practice. On the other hand, the various skills, roles and responsibilities–the individual's capacity to make decisions and take personal risks, personal attitudes towards obstacles and hostile environments, the will to change and to learn, etc.–that each person assumed or not created various degrees of power imbalance within the group. In some cases, fear and self-repression were stronger than the possibility of exploring new alternatives.

Thus, the need for spaces to exercise our rights, take care of our bodies and our lives began to take new and more complex dimensions. As GALF's membership began to grow, at the same time the increase of demand for services made us aware of other gaps. Although gynecological or legal services were already available in other spaces, including women and feminist groups, many of them were conceived and operated for a heterosexual public. Services that responded to domestic violence were designed with heterosexual couples in mind, where the husband/father was the aggressor; they did not consider the different forms of violence as a result of homophobia. Many lesbian users of these services had to mask their sexual orientation, either because of the lack of sensitivity of service providers or for fear of suffering discrimination. Legal cases related to custody of the children of lesbian mothers spoke volumes on homophobia as many judges tended to consider lesbians are morally inept for motherhood. Furthermore, how could the right to psychological, emotional and mental health be addressed without also considering the inadequate access to food, education, housing and work?

How could lesbians trust an important number of professionals who have a prejudiced or biased education towards homosexuality or lesbianism, or who admit that their knowledge on human sexuality is limited? We often saw signs of this in the quality and content of questions from the audience of students and professionals in presentations or debates in universities, hospitals and other centers that invited us as speakers. The favorable aspect of these spaces was that they also allowed us to find allies and contacts for our service referral directory, even though these were far too few.

The impact of multiple forms of discrimination on women with whom we worked demanded concrete responses from us. It led us to generate and improvise some services with the collaboration of individuals, mostly students, who had some training in basic listening skills and in offering alternative services while respecting safety and confidentiality. However, the services we have offered have been kept at an informal level, as we did not invest much time and resources in their provision or pay the necessary attention to give them greater structure, consistency and coverage.

GALF's grassroots work with the lesbian community was characteristic of its work until 1992. In 1996-97 GALF members organized some workshops for lesbians on various issues, but the weak turnout did not justify the necessary efforts to organize these events. In addition there are many more lesbian social spaces, real and virtual, than in the early years of GALF's existence. Moreover, organizations such as MHOL provide a level of services that GALF members could not afford to provide given constraints of time and resources. GALF's annual evaluation, which took place in January 2002, revisited the possibility of re-establishing activities addressing the lesbian community and tackling some issues that had been left pending. GALF is currently discussing how to address this area of work, how to change our organizational structure and how to motivate lesbians to organize around common objectives.

However, there is still resistance to including the provision of services as one of our explicit objectives. Legal, health and other services are related more to public responsibilities and structural changes than to GALF exclusively. Should the demand for these services increase, GALF will need to consider how to best respond: possibly by helping to improve services that already exist and by developing specific ways of cooperation with other organization such as MHOL and women's centers. In the current stage of GALF's development, the emphasis is on information services offered through *Labia* and on the internal strengthening of the organization through capacity building, leadership training and local advocacy for lesbians and human rights activists interested in these issues. We need to focus our energies on strategies that, in the long run, will help to reconstruct the fragmented and precarious existing social fabric. These are our realistic dreams!

CONCLUDING THOUGHTS: ALL THE BRIDGES THAT WE BUILD . . .

As pointed to in this article, organizing around a lesbian identity was a useful initial strategy. It helped us to visualize the discrimination and exclusion we faced as lesbians. It gave us the tools to transform the demeaning stereotypical images of lesbians into an empowered, defiant identity as feminist lesbians. However, as Phelan remarks, ". . . it has been part of the ideological function of the universalized 'subject' to remove individuals from their social locations and to present them as equal, autonomous agents, when in fact they are unequal and usually dominated" (Phelan, 1993, p. 778). Furthermore, a unitary, homogenizing identity often led to various forms of exclusion and discrimination of those, within and around our group, who were different from us, thus limiting the possibilities for building bridges with other groups and movements. Shifting identities were also perceived with fear and distrust. We did not recognize that our own subjectivity was "part of the terrain of possible change" (Phelan, 1993, p. 779). Indeed, our discourse against discrimination was not always consistent with our own internal practices.

> Proposals to identify or diagnose and combat specific discrimination will only be partially effective if we do not learn to exercise non-discriminatory practices regarding other people, to develop mechanisms that ensure plural participation, beginning at home. . . . Naming any form of discrimination does not exempt us from the responsibility of its practice. (Sevilla, 2000)

The analysis of these experiences teaches us that a universal lesbian identity must give way to more contextualized, multiple, and shifting identities that can account for the differences among us and for identities that are constantly under construction. Our participation in the process towards the World Conference Against Racism provided fertile grounds to reflect on how various forms of identity-based discrimination are interrelated and to initiate dialogue with various organizations and movements. The politics that these new interpretations call for is, likewise, more contextual and modest. It is not a politics based on a universal interpretation of discrimination and exclusion based on one more basic form of oppression that applies to everybody, at all times and places. It is a politics in which context and difference play a key role.

In the course of time, other lesbian groups in the region assumed various organizing strategies as they related to other movements: a separatist, autonomous, independent organization or one that interacted with (hetero-)feminist and mixed lesbian and gay groups. Each group assumed the individual and collective changes it had to, wanted to or could assume. They all had various successful experiences, as a result of the critical, challenging or transgressing attitudes towards established norms, overcoming fear, negative experiences or social disqualification. In this process, as part of the feminist movement, GALF fully assumed our rights and responsibilities in the construction of the Feminist Movement and its Coordinating Collective. We prioritized dialogue and the establishment of more constructive relationships, rather than promoting isolation or rupture.

The weakness or inability of GALF's structure to make it a more effective pressure group was also a factor that influenced some of the members in their decision to construct other bridges: with women's centers, MHOL, cultural spaces, etc. While there was a general consensus in our identification with the feminist movement, our alliances with MHOL were viewed with less clarity and were, as previously noted, the source of internal conflict in various periods of GALF's existence.

We learned by trial and error; we adapted some local and foreign experiences to our own needs and aims. We learned from our physical and materials limits. Now we know more about what to do and what not to, when, and with whom. There are also more activists and professional to work with, and more spaces, courses and seminars to share in and learn from. We do not need to reinvent the wheel but we do need to review some internal policies necessary for GALF's transition to a more formal organization and for getting financial support for our activities. There are concrete developments to explore and we still have the political perspective and will to take a chance, once again. The democratic process that began in Peru last year (2001) reaffirms our expectations, our rights and our responsibilities.

NOTES

1. *There are so many borders*
   Dividing people
   But for each border
   There is also a bridge
   This and all future references originally in Spanish have been translated by the authors of the present article.

   2. Currently in Peru, there is no legal recognition of same sex relationships nor any law that protects lesbians and gays from discrimination. While there are no laws that criminalize homosexuality the Civil Code mentions homosexuality as one of the grounds for requesting divorce.

3. The 1985 declaration included non discrimination at work on the grounds of sexual orientation.

4. At the time, Peru was under a state of emergency due to the increase of terrorism. One of the measures adopted by the government was the establishment of curfew hours in the city of Lima from 11 p.m. to 6 a.m. During these hours no one was allowed in the streets or other public spaces in Lima, unless one had a special police permit. There was no protection for anyone caught in public spaces during curfew hours and it was sufficient reason to be detained.

REFERENCES

Alvarez, S. (1990). *Engendering democracy in Brazil: Women's movement in transition politics*. New Jersey: Princeton University Press.

Anzaldúa, G. (1987). *Borderlands/La Frontera: The new Mestiza*. San Francisco: Spinsters/Aunt Lute.

Bunch, C. (1987). *Passionate politics*. New York: St. Martin's Press.

Bunch, C., & Hinojosa, C. (2000). *Lesbians travel the roads of feminism globally*. New York: Center for Women's Global Leadership.

Colectivo Coordinador de la Casa de la Mujer "La Morada." (1987, June 29). Lesbianas II-Carta al director. *APSI, 207,* 63.

Csömyei, C., & Palumbo, S. (1996). Las lunas y las otras. In M. Reinfelder (Ed.), *Amazon to Zami* (pp. 152-160). New York: Cassell Publishing Company.

GALF. (1997). *Ese secreto que tienes conmigo-Memorias del Galf*. Unpublished manuscript.

Irving, K. (1987, September). First Latin American and Caribbean Lesbian Conference. *Rites,* 12.

Lorenzo, M. (1985). Interview: A question of survival. *Cayenne-A Socialist Feminist Bulletin, 4,* 30-35.

Madden, R. M. A. (1996). Outraging public morality: The experience of a lesbian feminist group in Costa Rica. In M. Reinfelder (Ed.), *Amazon to Zami* (pp. 130-137). New York: Cassell Publishing Company.

Minh-Ha, Trinh T. (1988). Not you/like you: Post-colonial women and the interlocking questions of identity and difference. *Inscriptions, 3/4,* 71-77.

Phelan, S. (1993). (Be)coming out: Lesbian identity and politics. *Signs,* 18 (4), 765-790.

Rivera, C. F. (1996). Todas locas, todas vivas, todas libres: Chilean lesbians 1980-95. In M. Reinfelder (Ed.), *Amazon to Zami* (pp. 138-151). New York: Cassell Publishing Company.

Sevilla, R. (2000, August). *Mixed organizations*. Paper presented at the conference of the International Lesbian and Gay Association. Oakland, CA.

Vargas, V. (1993, October). *Untitled*. Paper presented at the anniversary meeting of Movimiento Homosexual de Lima. Lima, Peru.

Viñuales, O. (1999). *Identidades lésbicas*. Barcelona: Edicions Bellaterra.

Namaji:
Two-Spirit Organizing
in Montreal, Canada

Fiona Meyer-Cook
Diane Labelle

SUMMARY. This article traces the authors' involvement in Two-Spirit organizing in Montreal since 1995. The term "Two-Spirit" is often used by lesbian, gay, bisexual and transgendered (LGBT) people of Aboriginal descent in both the U.S. and Canada. The authors explore the multifaceted aspects of organizing within a Two-Spirit community. They begin with an examination of contemporary challenges facing Two-Spirit people within Canadian society and then provide several concrete examples of local organizing, ranging from the creation of an educational video on HIV/AIDS and participation in a collaborative project with a school of social work to national and international alliance-building. *[Article copies available for a fee from The Haworth Document Delivery Service: 1-800-HAWORTH. E-mail address: <docdelivery@haworthpress.com> Website: <http://www.HaworthPress.com> © 2004 by The Haworth Press, Inc. All rights reserved.]*

KEYWORDS. Two-Spirit, Canada, Montreal, aboriginal, video, social work, international

[Haworth co-indexing entry note]: "Namaji: Two-Spirit Organizing in Montreal, Canada." Meyer-Cook, Fiona, and Diane Labelle. Co-published simultaneously in *Journal of Gay & Lesbian Social Services* (Harrington Park Press, an imprint of The Haworth Press, Inc.) Vol. 16, No. 1, 2004, pp. 29-51; and: *Community Organizing Against Homophobia and Heterosexism: The World Through Rainbow-Colored Glasses* (ed: Samantha Wehbi) Harrington Park Press, an imprint of The Haworth Press, Inc., 2004, pp. 29-51. Single or multiple copies of this article are available for a fee from The Haworth Document Delivery Service [1-800-HAWORTH, 9:00 a.m. - 5:00 p.m. (EST). E-mail address: docdelivery@haworthpress.com].

Namaij (NA-MA-GEE): Ojibwe term for dignity, honour, respect and pride

TWO-SPIRITED PEOPLE OF TURTLE ISLAND

Today there are over one million Aboriginal people within Canada. There are 633 bands, with over 50 distinct languages spoken. Aboriginal People include those who are Status, Non-status, Metis and Inuit. There are 56,000 Inuit in Canada, many of whom live in the 55 communities across the North. About half of all Aboriginal people live in communities, sometimes called "reserves," the other half live in rural or urban centers. (Fleras & Elliott, 2002). In Quebec alone, there are approximately 73,000 Aboriginal people, living in 54 different communities, over one quarter of whom live in Montreal (Quebec Native Business Directory, 1998).

Many sociological and anthropological studies have confirmed that Aboriginal (First Nations, Metis and Inuit or Indigenous) tribes, prior to colonization, maintained the belief in more than two genders, and that some Nations even identified up to six different gender categories (Williams, 1986). Prior to colonization and the binary gender system implanted from Europe, Aboriginal people not only identified, but also had prescribed roles for such individuals. In most of the cases, such individuals were held in high esteem, being seen as having been given a gift from the Creator. Rather than being a taboo, or a reason to ostracize and isolate, what was different and unique about Two-Spirited people historically was often embraced, as their qualities where seen to add value and contribute to life within the communities. This article aims to contribute to a revaluing of Two-Spirited people by highlighting their often forgotten history and contemporary organizing efforts in Montreal, Canada. These organizing efforts are placed within the context of past and present oppression facing Aboriginal people in the Canadian context.

HISTORICAL BACKGROUND

Origin of the Word Two-Spirit

The term Two-Spirit is presently used to describe Aboriginal people with different roles or identities, including gays, lesbians, other genders (not-men, not-women), those of multiple genders (hermaphrodites and bisexuals), transvestites, transexuals, transgendered people, drag queens and butches (Jacobs, Thomas & Lang, 1997). The term is also used to refer to heterosexual people who have a unique place on the gender continuum, and who are seen to have a more expanded view of the world, as a result of their ability to mediate between, and see through the eyes of both sexes. Some of the medicine doctors of the past, for example, were heterosexual in their orientation, but were believed to have the gift of this "double vision," and would cross-dress for ceremonial purposes. Other people who cross-dressed, shamans or not, were known to have same-sex relationships. What is evident is that communities prior to colonization, were generally very inclusive and accepting of a range of sexual orientations and gender identities.

The term Two-Spirit or Two-Spirited was proposed in Minnesota in 1988 and coined in Winnipeg in 1990, at a gathering of the Native American/First Nation gay and lesbian conference. It is a generic term that was adopted in order to provide a modern means of regrouping Aboriginal people with other gender and sexuality identification, as well as to reawaken the spiritual nature of the role these people are meant to play in their communities.

The term Two-Spirit or Two-Spirited is not universally accepted by all Aboriginal people. One of the controversies stems from the caution against reducing the histories and rich and diverse traditions of Two-Spirited people into a common denominator. There is often concern and resistance against the term becoming equated with sexual orientation in and of itself. Being Two-Spirited is different from being gay or lesbian; it is not predominantly a description of one's sexual orientation, but rather one of gender identity and role. At the same time, prior to colonization, many Two-Spirited people did have socially sanctioned same-sex relationships. For example, consider the following observation of an ethnographer named Drydav who, on one day in 1812 arrived on Koniag Island in Alaska and observed that:

> there are among these people men with tattooed chins, carrying on solely female work, living always with women and similarly these having one and sometimes two husbands. They call these Achuceks. A Koniag who has a Achucek instead of a wife are considered lucky. (Hrdlicka, 1944, p. 79)

This understanding differs from the current use of terms such as gay and lesbian, which are ascribed to both people within a same sex relationship. The terms gay and lesbian also do not encompass the spiritual role towards the community and the responsibilities that were bestowed on Two-Spirit people in the past. These modern terms also cannot capture the sense that there were Two-Spirited people who were heterosexual. It can be difficult to understand sometimes, particularly since the historical understanding of the Tradition of Two-Spirited or Two-Spirit persons does not easily translate from Aboriginal languages into English.

Over 130 terms derived from Indigenous languages of North America describe people who historically did not fit into the typical binary gender categories of male or female (Roscoe, 1987). Although these vary, they often translate roughly into boy-girl (i.e., Blackfeet: *Sakwo'ma pi aki-kwan*) or man-woman (Tlingit: *Gaxtan*; Cree: *Aayahkwew*; Inuit: *Aranu'tiq*). Other terms defined an occupational role that did not fit the gendered norms, which usually went with a particular biological sex. For example, the Anishinaabe term for a Two-Spirited woman was *Okitcitakwe* (warrior woman), while the men were known as Ogokwe. The Dine/Navaho called Two-Spirited men *Nadle*, which means "weaver transformed," or "that which changes," or "he who transforms." Other terms described roles that were more sacred. The Yokuts term translated into "corpse handler," while a Blackfoot female born Two-Spirit was called *Natoyi* (sacred woman). The Dakota used the terms *Winkte* (double woman), while the Osage male was called *Mixu'ga* (moon instructed).

The search for the specific traditions and languages used prior to colonization has been an important tool in the resurgence of the knowledge of the multiplicity of traditions. There are still other people looking for the original words, trying to have conversations with the Elders and those who might remember–the inability to remember does not mean that there was not a word. In some communities today, a large number of members are practicing Seventh Day Adventists or Pentecostals. Trying to find someone who is willing to talk about sexual orientation and gender identity can be hard enough, but finding the buried traditions can be next to impossible.

Where Did It All Change?: Sexual Orientation/Gender Identity and the Early Days of the Canadian State

Some of the problems that Two-Spirited people face today such as being insulted, and made to feel unworthy, stem from the time when Christian morality replaced traditional values. Binary concepts prevailed in colonial days: good over evil, man over woman, Christianity over Tradition, white over brown, rich over poor, "man" over nature, and gender "conformity" over gender variance, were preached and instituted with both the bible and the gun. When the Europeans encountered a Peoples who thought in more circular ways, who valued the interrelationships of all living things, who celebrated and marked the "in between times" of nature, and whose artists and shamans regularly depicted the masks and paintings of shamans transforming, between the worlds of fish and sky, between man and woman, they were unable to comprehend the value in such ways of being. This incomprehension did not arise from an inability to understand, but from a difficulty in fitting these ways of being into a larger agenda. That which could not easily be co-opted for advancement and profit, that which stood in the way of their advancing agenda, was outlawed, warred upon and discredited. Racism, sexism, classism and heterosexism were some of the many tools that the Europeans used to thwart and control the Aboriginal cultures they encountered.

Audre Lorde (1984) has defined heterosexism as the belief in the inherent superiority of one form of loving over others, and by extension, the right to dominate. Heterosexism also bestows a system of advantages on heterosexuals and assumes that all people are or should be heterosexual and, therefore, excludes the needs, concerns, and life experiences of lesbian, gay, bisexual and transgender persons (Blumenfield, 1992). Heterosexism has its roots in a rigid biological view of gendered relations and sexuality, which dates back to a time when it was believed that sex should only be for procreation. These beliefs mask a set of culturally defined norms about gender, power and reproduction. Kinsman (1987, p. 25) writes that:

> Our sexuality has come to be defined by naturalistic notions to such a degree that the process of social organization is rendered invisible. . . . It must be stressed that powerful State and social policies lie behind the "naturalness" of heterosexuality.

The residential missionary schools provide a concrete example of how the institution of heterosexuality transformed the traditional roles of Two-Spirited people. These schools took three generations of Aboriginal children from Aboriginal homes, families and communities, and systematically tried to inculcate the belief in the superiority of patriarchal vs. matriarchal relations, the need for private land ownership, capitalism and the nuclear family. Exclusive heterosexuality and gender conformity were not only rewarded, but the very economic survival of young students was often linked to how well they adopted these norms. For example, in Duck Lake, Saskatchewan, a fifty-year commemorative book on St. Michael's residential missionary school, shows training for marriage as an explicit educational goal (Le Chevralier, 1944). The older boys were expected to build a small house on a piece of land chosen for them by the church before they could get out of school. The girls in the meantime were often placed in non-Native homes to work as servants, "to wait as house maids" for their future husbands. Academic studies had little place within these schools. Instead the missionaries, with the full backing of the Canadian government, constructed an educational system that was designed to give Aboriginal people only the basic skills in subsistence farming and living. It was then expected that boys, in their newly constructed patriarchal roles as property heads:

> would be taught the uselessness of traveling, of hunting and of roaming aimlessly, to cultivate the land, to make a *real* home thereon, and to find happiness in the *possession* of a good wife and in the raising of a family. (italics added) (Le Chevralier, 1944, p. 29)

The Church and State benefited in two distinct ways through this plan. First, by parceling out and confining couples to small tracts of land, and by not giving Aboriginal Peoples equal education or even equal tools to farm with, Aboriginal people were kept out of the growing economy. Secondly, large tracts of land previously used by Aboriginal Peoples, and desired by both the Church and State, became easier to grab. In this way, the church acted directly as an arm of the state using the discourse of morality and "family values" for their own ends.

By constructing possibilities for individual couples to find at least minimal happiness in a home within a marriage, the government was also able to avoid large scale social unrest. In a system which rewarded students heading for marriage and property with the means to survive economically, it is difficult to imagine where a Two-Spirited person would have fit. It would have been almost impossible for two women or two men to set up house together. In addition, laws were created to criminalize practices of cross dressing and transgender living: "In the 1880s for instance, as part of this mission, Canadian police forced a *berdache*[1] (sic) to wear men's clothes and to cut his hair" (Kinsman, 1987, p. 73).

Under the impact of colonization all gendered relations changed. Women, for example, used to have far more institutional decision-making power within communities (Etienne & Leacock, 1980). In the same way that women under colonization were forced to secure their economic stability and benefits through men, Two-Spirited people were forced to secure their survival and benefits through the institution of heterosexuality.

It is remarkable that despite the many massacres of Two-Spirited peoples across the Americas–e.g., the Spaniards' brutal use of dogs to tear apart the limbs of Indigenous men accused of sodomy, and the massacre of the Red Hands Society of male basket weavers in North America–those who had a unique gender identity and/or sexual orientation never disappeared, but rather went underground to survive. What is equally remarkable is that European states were not always averse to diversities of sexual orientation. For example, evidence indicates that prior to the Middle Ages, homosexuality was recognized and condoned, even by the Catholic Church (Ryan, 1998). However, the decline of European populations following the great plagues, created a situational environment where homosexual practices were perceived as threats to the survival of the population.

Colonization followed the plagues of Europe. The ensuing genocide through war and the smallpox epidemics put the very cultural survival of Aboriginal Peoples at risk. This may have also been an additional contributing factor in the changing views held by Aboriginal Peoples with respect to differently gendered individuals. In consequence, a once respected and valued element of Aboriginal life, became less valued over time, and in some cases eradicated from the life of some of our Nations. With the preponderance of the homophobic stances espoused by the dominant culture, it is surprising that any vestiges of this rich tradition have survived.

The re-emergence of Two-Spirit people within communities today is in a sense similar to the broader re-emergence of other traditions and sacred aspects of community life. In the same way that the drum, the sweat, the pipe and languages are re-emerging, Two-Spirit people are beginning to make their voices heard. Embracing and living openly as a Two-Spirited person today, whether this means living with a gender identity or sexual orientation that has historically been criminalized, psychiatrized and/or oppressed, can require much courage.

CONTEMPORARY SITUATION

In 1997 as part of her graduate degree in social work, Fiona interviewed nine Aboriginal people from across Quebec (Inuit, Mohawk, Dene, Ojibwe, and Naskapi) who self-identified as gay, lesbian, bisexual, or Two-Spirited. One person preferred not to use any labels at all, and felt that generally people use labels much too often these days. The interviewees were asked what strengths they felt they contributed to the strength of the communities they belonged to. The gifts they named were those of mediation, listening and sensitivity, strength and softness, keeping the balance, as well as the gift of being artists and educators.

Many people who are Two-Spirited are active in their communities today, and are using the gifts they have been given. Sometimes, they use their gifts in the service of community at the same time as dealing with insults, threats and intimidation. To understand why life can still be difficult for Two-Spirited people today, one has to look at the larger picture of current realities of Aboriginal peoples as a whole within the Canadian context.

Multiple Discrimination/Intersecting Oppressions and Two-Spirit People

While Canada and Canadians in general sit in an extremely privileged position in relation to most other countries around the world, Aboriginal people within Canada have not benefited from those conditions to the same degree. In 1998, a United Nation Human Rights Committee ruled that the treatment of Aboriginal Peoples within Canada stood in violation of international law and was the most pressing human rights issue facing Canadians. At the same time, while Canada has often been ranked number one on both the Human Development Index (HDI) and the Gender and Development Index, Aboriginal peoples on reserves were ranked sixty-third on the HDI (Fleras & Elliott, 2002).

Numerous challenges face Aboriginal people leading us to organize on many fronts. These have included the struggle for housing, land rights, and justice reform against police brutality and unfair sentencing procedures. Other challenges revolve around the struggle to improve economic and social development, including the eradication of poverty, homelessness, environmental racism and ill-health, which when combined lead Aboriginal people to have a shorter life expectancy than the average Canadian (Fleras & Elliott, 2002).

Other important struggles include dealing with the legacy of multi-generational trauma. Three generations of Aboriginal children were forcibly removed from their homes and brought up in church-run residential schools. They were often beaten for speaking their First languages, were taught to de-value their culture and families, and very often were physically and sexually abused by the priests and educators who ran these institutions. These schools operated for over 100 years, during which time their main aim was to completely eradicate Aboriginal cultural, familial, economic and spiritual life. The last residential school ceased operations in the 1970s.

There is a tremendous amount of pain still evident today as a result of devastating state policies and practices. Two-Spirited people today are dealing with the impacts of these practices, including ongoing discrimination against their sexual orientation and gender identity. Despite this history, Two-Spirited people continue to work in solidarity with other Aboriginal people for better economic and social conditions, in the fight against AIDS, as advocates for women and children, against state violence and land rights violations, and for many other vital needs. Unfortunately, the reverse is seldom true. Few leaders, Elders, activists and Aboriginal human rights advocates have stood by Two-Spirited people to model the kind of caring and inclusive communities that are envisioned and needed. Bones, one of the nine people interviewed by Fiona had this to say:

> I've been living for five years now out of the community. I've worked there almost every summer and I've still felt the tension there, so I don't know if it would be the best place to live really, because so many people know and so many people don't accept it. That's sad because this is your community. If this is where you want to live, you should be able to live there. (Meyer-Cook, 1998, p. 48)

Today, while there are Aboriginal families and individuals who continue to have an understanding of Two-Spirited people's value in contributing to the circle of diverse and healthy communities, in many more cases, this knowledge and understanding has disappeared. We have sometimes been accused of making up this diverse past in order to feel good about ourselves. When this lack of understanding of pre-colonial history is combined with the aggravated factors of racism, poverty, the legacy of multi-generational trauma and the full impact of colonization, Two-Spirited people today can quickly become vulnerable to the strains of multiple forms of discrimination.

Particular Challenges Facing Two-Spirited People Today

In September 2001, at the United Nations World Conference Against Racism (WCAR), Brazil put forward a motion to introduce the following paragraph into the governmental WCAR document, urging

States and non-governmental organizations to acknowledge that individuals who are victims of racism, racial discrimination, xenophobia and related intolerance, in many cases may also face discrimination based on sexual orientation, and calls upon States, in consultation with competent non-governmental organizations to, when appropriate, develop, implement and improve specific policies and programmes to effectively address this form of multiple discrimination. (par. 68, World Conference Secretariat, 2002)

Today's Two-Spirited people face incredible obstacles. They are of two worlds, the world of the differently gendered, and the world of being Native. In essence, they are subject to multiple oppressions. As part of a minority based on gender or sexuality differences, they are shunned by both the dominant external culture, as well as among their own communities. As people of Native heritage, they are oppressed and influenced by the surrounding dominant culture. For Two-Spirited people born in a woman's body, they face yet a third form of oppression based on gender. Taking this into consideration, sound identity formation is an upward struggle.

To achieve a sound identity, Two-Spirited people need to simultaneously follow two tracts of identity formation: first as Native people or people of a minority group; and second, as people who are differently gendered. According to Cass (1984), the coming out process for gays and lesbians involves six stages: identity confusion, comparison, tolerance, acceptance, pride and synthesis. Identity formation, as a Native person, is dependent upon surrounding values, which ". . . play a significant role in creating and defining parameters as to expected cultural roles and norms" (Walters, 1997, p. 51). As Brown (1997) explains,

Euro-American spirituality has had a significant impact on the internalization of negative attitudes toward GAIs [Gay American Indians] among Indian peoples. In turn, the negative attitudes that non-gay Indians express verbally or non-verbally have an impact on GAI identity development. (p. 49)

Among many of today's aboriginal tribes, there is a fear of homosexuality, in part for its difference, but also because of reminders of the "the old ways" (Brown, 1997). Residential schools have played an important role in the development of this fear. These schools were created for the purpose of "taking the Indian out of the Indian," creating shame based values around anything deemed Native: language, belief systems, traditions, ceremonies, etc. . . . . These were replaced with Judeo-Christian values, which viewed sexual expression as only acceptable for procreation, and same-sex sexual contact as taboo. Adding to present day fear of same-sex relations is the negative memory association many survivors of residential school have with respect to the sexual abuse, often same-sex in nature, that they endured while in residential schools. As such, Two-Spirited people are seen in the same light as sin and sexual abusers.

In worlds that shun their existence, they become invisible (Little Thunder, 1997). Surviving becomes equated with on-going trauma and having to contend with on-going losses related to their freedom, cultural identity, gender identity, sexuality, security and physical safety for themselves and their loved ones. Also related are losses of family and family support, and the denial of the self. The result is that

> Many of the two-spirited of new, have moved off the reservation and into big metropolitan cities in an effort to find a community for themselves only to succumb to poverty, racism, sexism, and suicide. Some even have to undergo a new type of cultural genocide in order to become a part of today's gay, lesbian, bisexual and transgendered movement. (Slivers, 2001, p. 2)

Another particular challenge concerns Two-Spirited youths, who are subject to the homophobia that also threatens their non-Aboriginal counterparts. Over 90% of LGBT youth report that they sometimes or frequently hear homophobic remarks in their school and 36% report hearing homophobic remarks from faculty or school staff (Gay And Lesbian Educators, 2000). LGBT youth are almost twice as likely as their non-gay peers to be threatened with or injured by a weapon at school; they are also more than four times as likely to skip whole days of school out of fear.

Out of isolation and desperation, these sexual minority youth develop various behaviours as means of adapting to the stress of their lives, including drug use. In addition, these young Two-Spirited people often become subjected to the same disadvantages and dangers facing other minority youth living in urban areas, including increased sexual risks and violence. In turn, these sexual risks increase their risk of HIV/AIDS infection.

As the AIDS epidemic hit the communities, many Two-Spirited people did not have access to the kind of health education and resources that could speak about healthy sexuality and lifestyles for Two-Spirited people. Over the years great strides have been made by a number of Aboriginal people across the country in the AIDS field, to educate and sensitize community health representatives, nurses, and community members. More work needs to be done in the prisons. The fact that Aboriginal people have a higher rate of incarceration, combined with a higher rate of HIV/AIDS in the prisons, puts Aboriginal people more at risk. According to Laverne Monette who has been working in Ontario with Two-Spirited people, and Aboriginal people with HIV/AIDS, the link between homophobia and AIDS is something that puts all Aboriginal people at risk (personal communication, 1999). For as long as people think they cannot contract HIV if they are not involved in a same sex relationship, then the numbers of AIDS cases across the country will continue to rise.

Two-Spirited men who have same sex relationships continue to be vulnerable to HIV infection. It may be that when people are devalued in their own communities, and when they leave for the cities where racism continues to marginalize them, the aggravated factors of multiple discrimination may result in a weakening of their ability to make healthy lifestyle choices. Suicide becomes the only option for many, especially among youth. Suicide among Native youth is several times greater than for other adolescents (Department of Indian Affairs and Northern Development, 2000). As Slivers (2001) notes, "suicide is a very real and very prevalent problem within both Native American and queer communities. Couple the two together and it's amazing any Native American queers survive their adolescence" (p. 4).

With few Two-Spirit people knowing where and how to gain access to "Two-Spirit friendly" Elders, role models, healthy lifestyle alternatives and inclusive cultural spaces, many "fall through the cracks" and end up on city streets, living in poverty with poorer health and with greater risk of becoming lost and in pain. Whether one chooses to stay in one's community or "on the rez," or to migrate to the urban centres, at this time within the Canadian state, being a Two-Spirited person is, for a great many people, a very difficult and challenging state of being.

Even on a professional front, social workers and therapists are not always sensitive to GLBT issues. Fewer yet would understand the complex world of Two-Spiritedness. The risk is high that even sensitive interventions would equate Two-Spiritedness with sexual orientation, and little attention would be given to the spiritual/role component of these special beings.

Today's Context: Québec and The Rights of Gays and Lesbians

In addition to the perception of Two-Spirited people in their own communities, differently gendered people are influenced by the values of the dominant culture that surrounds them. In Quebec, Two-Spirited people have witnessed great changes with respect to rights for gays and lesbians, which may not impact on their lives on the reserve, but offer greater freedom off reserve. This can be troublesome, since it establishes fertile ground for having to make choices between being gay/lesbian/bisexual or transgendered, and being Aboriginal.

Quebec is the first Canadian province to recognize the rights of gays and lesbians in its anti-discrimination clause of the Charter of Rights and Freedoms in 1977. It was only in 1982 that there was a similar inclusion in the Canadian Charter of Rights and Freedoms. In June of 1999, the National Assembly of the province passed law C32, which gave lesbian and gay couples the same status as common law couples (or more precisely "conjoints de faits"), with respect to social and administrative matters, but fell short of granting equal rights with respect to legal, fiscal and inheritance matters. In July 2000, the federal law C-23 came into effect, granting same sex couples the right to be recognized as a couple for taxation purposes, but still denied same-sex couples the right to marry, adopt, or have shared parental rights.

In November 2001, Bill C-11 was passed by the Canadian Senate, granting immigration rights to the partners of same-sex couples. Equality for Gays and Lesbians Everywhere (EGALE), Canada's national LGBT advocacy organization, along with others, are continuing to question the one year cohabitation requirement before couples are recognized as common law spouses (EGALE, 2001). Advocates are also continuing to press for greater protection for the rights of refugees who seek asylum because of persecution based on their sexual orientation or gender identity.

Then on November 28, 2001, a federal minister stated that there was unanimous agreement among federal, provincial and territorial justice ministers to add sexual orientation to federal hate propaganda/hate crimes laws. Unfortunately it took the brutal murder of a gay Vancouver resident, Aaron Webster, to elicit this federal response.

In December 2001, as the Superior Court of Quebec was being asked to rule on the rights of same sex couples to marry in the case of Michael Hendricks and Rene Leboeuf, the government of Quebec proposed the civil union bill. Though this proposed law will further guarantee the rights of gay and lesbian couples in the province, as written, it will fall short of granting full equality to gays and lesbians. The proposed law will create a union strictly for same sex couples, not equal in rights and obligations prescribed by marriage and other recognized unions of opposite sex couples, and provides no recognition of families headed by same sex parents. At present, for couples who have conceived a child through insemination or surrogacy, only the biological parent has rights. In the advent of this parent's death, children's rights to stay with the nonbiological parent are not assured, nor are the nonbiological parent's obligations towards the child. With no legal and social recognition, these families are discriminated against, and in particular, the children are penalized.

At present, a commission is set to begin hearing testimony with respect to this proposed law, and there is hope that it will be modified before it reaches the assembly. However, such a law will not apply to Two-Spirited people living on reserves, because band governments have the justifiable right to establish their own laws of governance. Each Nation needs to develop its own set of values within its own developmental process. Obliging them to adopt an external system is a repeat of history. At present, in Quebec, many people on the reserves have adopted a negative view of homosexuality, which has been problematical for all individuals with gender identifications that differ from the societal norm.

Yet for Two-Spirited people, the progress being made on the Quebec front creates a new dilemma. In the absence of reclaimed value for differently gendered people, Two-Spirited people will have more rights off than on reserves. How will this affect their choice of residency? How will these people who choose to live off reserve guarantee their spiritual development? Will they be forced to choose between being differently gendered or being Aboriginal? Will the band councils harden their position against Aboriginal people who are gay and lesbian, and consequently other gender variances, by ascribing a non-Aboriginal value to the quest for gay rights? How will Two-Spirited people regain their right to live and work as equal members of their community? These are some of the problems to be addressed by this new generation of Two-Spirited people living in Quebec.

EMPOWERMENT AND COMMUNITY ORGANIZING

The modern Two-Spirit movement emerged in the 1960s, with the creation of an organization called the Gay American Indians (GAI) in

San Francisco. This moment marked the beginnings of the study of gender issues and identity from Aboriginal perspectives, challenging the previously espoused beliefs of non-Aboriginal researchers. In the 1960s, it was noted by researchers that unlike non-Aboriginal people, few Aboriginals would reject family members because they are different (Brown, 1997) a fact attributed to the traditional value that every member of the community plays a vital role in the survival of the whole. Differences are *not* singled out or put down by those who have a more traditional understanding of Aboriginal values.

Today there are vast differences between communities. In some communities Two-Spirited people are relatively at ease. Others sometimes feel that it is not safe to express themselves fully, and, therefore, attempt to keep a low profile. Others develop strategies of simply not caring what others think, and try to live their lives as best as they can, feeling entitled to be in the community. In short, depending on which community one lives in, living as a person with a sexual orientation or gender identity that has been discredited and shamed through the process of colonization, can be stressful and exhausting.

Openness about one's sexuality or gender identification is not always welcome on the reserve, and has resulted in many young women and men having to leave their home communities. In some of the worst cases, within a few Nations, as well as within urban and rural areas, differently gendered people have been insulted, beaten and even killed. When people have to leave their home communities, they also have to leave behind their communities' value systems, their own Nations' spiritual traditions, their language and other vital aspects of their culture. That being said, there are also numerous examples of individuals who have felt accepted by their families, and by many people within their communities. There are also many stories still in the making of families coming to terms with, and transforming their own understandings.

Two-Spirit People in and Around Montreal Mobilize for Change

> Two-Spirited beings are strengthened by and should be entitled to support, being able to talk and grieve, the ability to participate in various groups, attending Two-Spirited gatherings, learning about one's culture and traditions, having a spiritual view towards obstacles and development of personal interests. Together these help towards the development of a sense of oneself and pride in who one is. (Meyer-Cook, 1998, p. 30)

Bearing this belief in mind, we have been engaged in Two-Spirit organizing in and around Montreal. Three projects are highlighted in what follows: the Video Project, Gathering Together, and Project Interaction. Local organizing efforts are undertaken in conjunction with more regional and international collaborations, which will be discussed further below.

The Video Project

Fiona's first contact with information about the history of the Two-Spirited tradition was with Marcel Dubois, a Metis epidemiologist and Director of the Urban Aboriginal Aids Awareness Project, a program that operated out of the Native Friendship Center of Montreal. Initial discussions focused on the homophobia of health care providers and how it contributed to the difficulties of working on HIV/AIDS in Aboriginal communities. His own practice experience and research demonstrated higher HIV infection rates for Aboriginal peoples of Canada, and showed that Aboriginal men who had sex with men accounted for (at the time) 75% of all Aboriginal people with AIDS (Marcel Dubois, personal communication, 1997). He was engaged in a project to educate health care providers in Northern and remote communities, to issues of HIV/AIDS and Two-Spirited people, and how both were interconnected.

Though he did outreach to these health organizations and distributed a monthly newsletter to all Aboriginal communities in Quebec, he voiced the need to find other means of getting the message across. At first, Fiona and Marcel Dubois contemplated using theatre as a medium, but the logistics proved too difficult to manage. With the arrival of a young film student, their thoughts turned to another communication tool, and the idea of an educational video was born.

The plan was to create an Aboriginal video about HIV/AIDS that explicitly talked about Two-Spirited people, homophobia and its impact, and a vision for greater inclusion. It was agreed that a larger audience could be reached if we addressed Two-Spirited issues alongside heterosexual ones. With a zero budget, the video was planned, organized and Aboriginal people were filmed discussing HIV/AIDS. Some time was then spent time editing the product.

Despite interest from the social services community in this training tool, it has not been possible to secure funding from Health Canada to complete the project. The video remains in "rough" draft form. However, the film is being regularly used as an educational tool. Fiona receives regular requests to show it in social work classrooms, among other venues. There is still hope that a final version can be prepared and distributed to different Community Health Representatives (CHR) in the North and rural areas.

Gathering Together

Another important organizing strategy has been simply gathering together. Ruby, gifted organizer and crafts woman, with a unique talent for bringing people together hosted in 1996 a Two-Spirited barbecue, which attracted some 25 individuals. This first gathering provided an opportunity to create personal links, and led to the creation of the first Two-Spirited organization of Montreal.

The following summer, a group of us (six or seven) spent several late nights making traditional crafts, while we listened to K.D. Lang singing to us in the background, and shared our personal stories. We wove dreamcatchers, beaded pins and key chains and peyote stitched pen and lighter covers. The purpose was to sell these items at the upcoming gay pride in order to begin raising funds for a Two-Spirited gathering. In August of 1997, our Two-Spirited group (10 or 12 of us) marched openly in the Gay Pride March of Montreal, carrying our hand made banner, and singing and drumming. For some of us, this was a truly proud moment, but for others, it gave way to fear of becoming targets of harassment. Annie, one of the women interviewed by Fiona expressed the following:

> I still have a lot of fears, of homophobic fears, like with the family. But an interesting thing happened when I was at the parade. I saw some people from my hometown. I went over to Suzy and I said "What am I going to do? I see these two people from my hometown." And she said "Why don't you just wave at them?" So we were passing by and I just waved at them and smiled. So it was a big step. It was really scary. I don't know what's going to happen, if they're going to question. And then I saw a lot of people that I know. So it was really quite interesting just to be there. (Meyer-Cook, 1998, p. 48)

In December 1997, our funding efforts were aided by the addition of funds donated from Kanesatake and Kahnawake Social Services. Dr. Terry Tafoya, a Taos Pueblo storyteller, sexologist and diversity educator came to our gathering and worked with Two-Spirited people and their family members. He provided us with an excellent history of traditions of Two-Spirited people, and through shared discussion, helped us deal with the shame and oppression imposed on us in our lives.

Part of the importance of such gatherings is to reverse isolation. By sharing and meeting more people, we are able to gain strength in our individual lives. These gatherings also provide us with an opportunity to come together and mirror the kind of balance keeping and inclusive values we are calling on our communities to demonstrate. If we can't begin within ourselves, how can we expect any other outside entity to "get it together"?

For a few years, we maintained our presence at Pride through our booth, but we did not march again. Some members, like Ruby, left Montreal, and others became involved with other organizations fighting for rights. As our numbers dwindled, the few that were left felt less like being visible. We keep imagining and hoping that some day, we will have a large presence again. In our everyday lives, we have come across many Two-Spirited people, and have realized that they are not aware of the attempts made to get together. We are often unknown to each other and swallowed up by the larger gay/lesbian/transgendered community, and because of the on-going lack of resources, we often miss the opportunity to bring people in on an event.

Project Interaction: Working in Coalition

For the past three years, we have been members of the steering committee for Project Interaction, the gay, lesbian, bisexual and Two-Spirited initiative of the McGill School of Social Work. As part of a working circle within the project, we identified some objectives and outlined a plan of activities for Two-Spirited people. Three priorities were identified: the need to build links between local Two-Spirited people, the need to increase awareness of Two-Spirited people among counselors, health providers and educators, and the need to reduce discrimination, oppression and lateral violence towards Two-Spirited people in our communities.

As a result, a "Wellness Gathering" is scheduled for this spring, and is timed for the spring solstice. The time was chosen specifically because of the "in between time," and it is hoped that it will become an annual event. We also hope to secure funding for future gatherings, so that we may provide travel grants to individuals in remote communities.

In the interim, individuals continue to work on the issues affecting Two-Spirited people. Suzy Goodleaf, a Mohawk psychologist, has been active in counseling and teaching about Two-Spirited people. Recently, she teamed up with another Aboriginal trainer to give a six-day workshop on trauma and healing to Two-Spirited people. This event was sponsored by the Inter Tribal Health Authority of Nanaimo, B.C. Diane has developed a program to deal with homophobia in schools, and is active in the Lesbian Mothers Association of Quebec, lobbying for parental and family rights. Several other members of the original group that first gathered together in 1996 continue to actively work and teach about Two-Spirited issues.

In 2002, a Two-Spirited group also began operation at the Native Friendship Center, in response to a long expressed need to do so. However, there is debate as to whether or not the location is conducive to creating necessary safety for Two-spirited participants. Warren, one of the Two-Spirit people interviewed by Fiona stated that:

> A lot of people don't go to the friendship centre because they're afraid of it getting back to their home. Having a two-spirit drop-in centre in another location from the friendship centre would be good. . . . At the same time, other people have felt it's a good sign that there is now a group within the Friendship centre, and hope to see more groups operate out of other Friendship centres across the country. (Meyer-Cook, 1998, p. 52)

It will be important for us to always ask ourselves the questions: "Who is not here?" "Whose voices are not being heard?" We rarely see or hear from older Two-Spirited people, and we have to question why they are so invisible. We also need to think about what it is we can do to give support to the Two-Spirited youth, especially those living in more isolated or remote communities.

While local organizing efforts of different groups and individuals are helping to create a better climate for Two-Spirited people, many of the underlying social problems, for example, the higher risk of HIV infection, and a higher than national average risk for suicide, are still there. Therefore, additional strategies are needed to advocate towards change, not only for those who remain most adversely affected, and most at risk, but also for those who dream of a time when Two-Spirited people are really considered part of the circle. In the meantime, much can be learned by creating bridges with others that are working towards the eradication of all forms of discrimination.

Dimensions: National Consultations and International Linkages

The United Nations World Conference Against Racism provided a unique and important opportunity to take the issues of multiple discrimination to the world stage. Canada supported the inclusion of paragraphs calling for governments around the world to implement programs and activities to remedy the negative impacts of intersecting discrimination based on racism and homophobia. Concretely, these texts need to be followed up with more opportunities for those facing multiple discrimination within Canada to speak with each other.

In February 2002, as a follow up to the WCAR, Equality for Gays And Lesbians Everywhere (EGALE) Canada, held a National Consultation with Aboriginal people and people of various cultural communities affected by racism and homophobia combined. Out of this consultation, a number of preliminary recommendations emerged. However, because the consultation was organized too quickly and included a very small source of input, many important voices were missing. As a result, one of the recommendations included a call for a national consultation of Aboriginal Two-Spirited people, to be able to develop further strategies and recommendations, as Aboriginal people.

Many important players involved in Two-Spirit organizing and wellness were also missing from the table. An interest was expressed on the part of those present in continuing the dialogue and with a larger number of people continuing to look at what type of partnership could be formed with EGALE. This partnership would be truly reciprocal, with aboriginal people informing EGALE about treaty rights and inter-jurisdictional issues, and with EGALE on the other hand possibly informing us about the human rights code and strategies to lobby and advocate for LGBT rights. EGALE's access to a database of those working to reduce homophobia was also a related recommendation. At the same time, having more access in between the Aboriginal communities and increased networking across Turtle Island were perceived to be outside the domain of EGALE, but important to pursue through other means.

More specifically, the particular ways of working, the media used that reflect the unique cultural and linguistic heritages of the Aboriginal Nations were seen as something important to share from region to region and Nation to Nation. Within Canada, there presently exists an organization called Two-Spirited People of the First Nations. This organization, has regional, national and international linkages. Participants at the EGALE consultation recognized the vital role of this organization in building national linkages. They also felt it to be essential to hold further discussions with people across the country in a way that includes this organization, before further recommendations for partnerships with EGALE, can be made. Strengthening linkages with other Aboriginal organizations was also suggested during the consultation. These linkages can be made through, for example, writing to the Gender Division of the Assembly of First Nations (AFN), and writing a proposal for collaboration to the Aboriginal Healing Foundation (AHF).

As we gathered from across the country and began talking about strategies for change, it became clear that too few organizations across the country are mandated to deal with the impacts of heterosexism and oppression on Two-Spirited people's lives. Often, the work of dealing with oppression and sensitizing people to lateral violence and homophobia falls on the shoulders of those working in the field of HIV/AIDS. There are multiple issues that Two-Spirit people face as a result of the intersection of discriminations: poorer health and HIV/AIDS are only two examples. Following in the steps of the WCAR, one of the first steps Canada could take to redress the grievances caused by multiple discrimination would be to fund a National Two-Spirited consultation, so that more people could contribute to our understanding of the specific manifestations of multiple discrimination, could voice their grievances, and could make suggestions towards remedies.

CONCLUSION

In summary, the term Two-Spirit reflects two basic principles: first, it identifies all Aboriginal individuals who have a gender identification that is different from the binary view of male and female; and second, the term encapsulates the notion that their role and identity are grounded in spirituality and not on sexual orientation. Prior to colonization, these individuals would be identified early in their development, and then taken under the guidance of an elder who would teach them about their special nature and their role in ceremonies. This allowed for identity and spiritual development. The process of colonization has diluted the consciousness of the spiritual nature of these special people: very few people know, for example, that up until the late 1880s the Sac and Fox tribes still held honor dances for Two-Spirited people (Williams, 1986). In the absence of elders who can teach about this rich history, there is little hope of reclaiming traditions of the past.

Five hundred years of colonization have wreaked havoc on the gendered lives of Aboriginal peoples radically transforming First Nations and Inuit relationships with respect to sexuality, gender and sexual orientation. This transformation has impacted: gender assigned roles and responsibilities, such as the clan mothers system; the role of parenting; and women's role in teaching and transmitting values to the young; as well as the roles and responsibilities previously accorded to Two-Spirited people. Europeans also introduced the current marriage and kinship system as well as divorce laws; they decided who could marry, and what relationships would be socially sanctioned.

We cannot undo the damage of colonization on traditions, but we can re-define them within the reality of today's world. Today, there are yearly gatherings of Two-Spirited people held in the U.S. and Canada in alternating years. The purpose of such gatherings is multi-fold. These gatherings are means of regrouping those whom history has marginalized within the non-Aboriginal as well as the Aboriginal world. They are also a way to build a sense of solidarity and to incite pride and acceptance of the Creator's gift. The gatherings especially provide a means of exploring and reclaiming our culture and spirituality. To do so requires that much effort be put towards teaching of pre-colonialist Aboriginal traditions surrounding gender identification, of the changes that have ensued as a result of colonialism, and of the reclaiming of traditional Aboriginal values of inclusiveness and diversity as a means of keeping the circle strong.

NOTE

1. Originally a French term, "berdache" translates into "boy kept for unnatural purposes." While the term was in use at one point in time, it is now considered to have pejorative connotations.

REFERENCES

Blumenfeld, W. (1992). *Homophobia: How we all pay the price*. Boston: Beacon Press
Brown, L.B. (Ed.). (1997). *Two spirit people*. Binghamton, NY: Harrington Park Press.
Cass, V.C. (1984). Homosexual identity formation: Testing a theoretical model. *Journal of Sex Research, 20*, 143-167.
Department of Indian Affairs and Northern Development. (2000). *Northern indicators 2000*. Ottawa: Minister of Indian Affairs and Northern Development.

Equality for Gays And Lesbians Everywhere (EGALE). (Winter, 2001). *Info EGALE.* Ottawa: Author.

Etienne, M., & Leacock, E.B. (1980). *Women and colonization.* New York: Praeger Publishers.

Fleras, A., & Elliott, J.L. (2002). *Engaging diversity: Multiculturalism in Canada.* Scarborough, ONT: Nelson Thomson Learning.

Gay And Lesbian Educators. (2000). *Gay and Lesbian Educators of British Columbia.* Vancouver: Quebecor World.

Hrdlicka, A. (1944). *The anthropology of Kodiak Island.* New York: AMS Press.

Jacobs, S.E., Thomas, W., & Lang, S. (Eds.). (1997). *Two spirit people: Native American gender identity, sexuality and spirituality.* Chicago: University of Illinois Press.

Kinsman, G. (1987). *The regulation of desire: Sexuality in Canada.* Montreal: Black Rose Books.

Le Chevralier, J. (1944). *St Michael's School: Trials and progress (sic) of an Indian school 1894-1944.* Duck Lake: Provincial Archivist of the Oblate Fathers of Alberta and Saskatchewan.

Little Thunder, B. (1997). I am a Lakota womyn. In S.E. Jacobs, W. Thomas & S. Lang (Eds.), *Two spirit people: Native American gender identity, sexuality and spirituality* (pp. 203-209). Chicago: University of Illinois Press.

Lorde, A. (1984). *Sister outsider: Essays and speeches.* Trumansburg, NY: Crossing Press.

Meyer-Cook, F. (1998). *The Two-spirit papers: The impact of heterosexism and homophobia on Inuit and First Nations peoples lives.* Unpublished MSW research report, McGill University, Montreal, Quebec.

Quebec Native Business Directory. (1998). Wendake, Quebec: Indiana Marketing.

Roscoe, W. (1987). Bibliography of Berdache (sic) and alternative gender roles among Native American Indians. *Journal of Homosexuality, 14* (3/4), 168.

Ryan, B. (1998). *S'accepter comme gai ou lesbienne: Pour en finir avec la honte.* In Ministère de la Santé et Services Sociaux (Ed.), *Adapter nos interventions aux réalités homosexuelles* (pp. 41-51). Quebec City: Ministère de la Santé et services sociaux.

Slivers, Y. (2001). *Two hearted beings.* Retrieved February 1, 2001 from <http://www.twohearted.com>.

Walters, K.L. (1997). Urban lesbian and gay American identity: Implications for mental health service delivery. In L. B. Brown (Ed.), *Two spirit people* (pp. 43-65). Binghamton, NY: Harrington Park Press.

Williams, W.L. (1986). *The spirit and the flesh: Sexual diversity in American Indian culture.* Boston: Beacon Press.

World Conference Secretariat. (2002). *Durban declaration and action program.* Geneva: Office of the United Nations High Commissioner for Human Rights.

Yoesuf:
An Islamic Idea
with Dutch Quality

Omar Nahas

SUMMARY. The author relies on his own experience as a researcher and community organizer to discuss a Muslim response to homosexuality in the Netherlands. The article provides detailed information on the work of the Yoesuf Foundation, a community organization that aims to bridge this knowledge gap between the Muslim community and Dutch society, while specifically focusing on battling homophobia and xenophobia. Following a brief introduction of Yoesuf, the author discusses the organizing strategy adopted by the Foundation, including the emphasis placed on building alliances with international Muslim organizations as well as with local social service providers. *[Article copies available for a fee from The Haworth Document Delivery Service: 1-800-HAWORTH. E-mail address: <docdelivery@haworthpress.com> Website: <http://www.HaworthPress.com> © 2004 by The Haworth Press, Inc. All rights reserved.]*

KEYWORDS. The Netherlands, Dutch, Muslim, Islam, xenophobia, homophobia, community organizing, Yoesuf

---

[Haworth co-indexing entry note]: "Yoesuf: An Islamic Idea with Dutch Quality." Nahas, Omar. Co-published simultaneously in *Journal of Gay & Lesbian Social Services* (Harrington Park Press, an imprint of The Haworth Press, Inc.) Vol. 16, No. 1, 2004, pp. 53-64; and: *Community Organizing Against Homophobia and Heterosexism: The World Through Rainbow-Colored Glasses* (ed: Samantha Wehbi) Harrington Park Press, an imprint of The Haworth Press, Inc., 2004, pp. 53-64. Single or multiple copies of this article are available for a fee from The Haworth Document Delivery Service [1-800-HAWORTH, 9:00 a.m. - 5:00 p.m. (EST). E-mail address: docdelivery@haworthpress.com].

INTRODUCTION

The Netherlands is introducing new rights for minorities in a rapid tempo. Gay and lesbian married couples can adopt Dutch children, and people are debating changing the national anthem to answer to society's multicultural needs. Within this rapidly evolving context there are various points of friction between the Muslim community and homosexual women and men. The need to know the "other" grows out of daily experiences in schools and the workplace where gays and lesbians are in regular contact and communication with Muslims. Indeed, there have recently been discussions on the national level of issues and problems arising between Muslim youth and gays and lesbians. The discussions, which were prevalent in the Dutch media in the period between 1990 and 1997, were characterized by fear, judgement and rejection of the "other." Information about one group was not available to the other group, and it was in this context that the Yoesuf foundation saw light in 1998. Since then, the Yoesuf Foundation has striven to bridge this knowledge gap between the Muslim community and Dutch society, while specifically focusing on battling homophobia and xenophobia.

In this article, I will discuss the work of the Yoesuf Foundation, specifically highlighting the aspects of empowerment and solidarity that are embedded within our work. Following a brief introduction of Yoesuf, I will discuss the organizing strategy that we have adopted. I will then briefly discuss the alliances that the Foundation has attempted to foster with international Muslim organizations as well as with local social service providers. I will conclude with a discussion of some of the future directions that Yoesuf hopes to take in the upcoming years. Throughout this paper, I contend that for a lasting acceptance of the other and for long-term social change, such solidarity and empowerment are essential ingredients in the struggle towards the emancipation of homosexual Muslims within a primarily non-Muslim context. Moreover, I maintain that it is essential to adopt strategies that are culturally relevant to Muslims living within a primarily non-Muslim context; from such strategies, a culturally-relevant emancipatory model can be born.

YOESUF FOUNDATION: ORIGINS AND ACTIVITIES

The Yoesuf Foundation is a research and information centre on Islam and homosexuality, based in the Netherlands. The Foundation is currently composed of three staff members, 15 volunteers, and an active advisory board consisting of 14 members. Establishing Yoesuf was not the easiest endeavour. The founders of the organization, two gay friends, a Muslim and a humanist, reached out to representatives of the Islamic community and others in Dutch society. An advisory board was formed consisting of Islamic leaders and members of parliament. This initial group wrote the foundational statement of the organization. Because of Yoesuf's intention to present information that would appeal to a large segment of the population, it was clear at the outset that the Foundation should consist of homosexuals, heterosexuals, Muslims and non-Muslims who are concerned with the common issue of gaining information on Islam and homosexuality.

Gaining acceptance from other gay and lesbian Dutch organizations was not a problem. Indeed, these organizations offered the Foundation a physical space within their premises. While appreciative of these offers, the Foundation chose to be independent of Islamic and Dutch gay and lesbian organizations, in order to maintain its unique character as an organization specialised in providing information on Islam and homosexuality.

Yoesuf's main goal is to advance a better understanding of each other's lifestyles, religious background and sexual orientation. In order to realize this goal, Yoesuf started a three-year project entitled "Islamic Studies on Homosexuality." The fundamental aim of these studies is to develop a culturally acceptable emancipatory model from the Islamic point of view on how to deal with contemporary issues on homosexuality. In addition to reviewing the existing literature, the Foundation initiated Study Days, described below, in order to gather information from both sides: the Islamic scholars and the Dutch social services providers in general. These Study Days were essential activities in fostering a dialogue between Dutch social service providers and the mainstream Islamic community.

As a foundation to these Study Days, it was necessary to first understand the viewpoints of homosexual men and women from Muslim backgrounds living in the Dutch context. In order to do so, the Foundation initiated discussion groups and workshops that were premised on the understanding that gays and lesbians of Islamic background need to develop more self-esteem and to feel that they are an integral part of society. In fact, self-help groups in mainstream Dutch homosexual organizations have shown us that gay and lesbian Muslims keep repeating the same questions about their sexual identity and their religion without being able to carry these questions further. Their discussions with other gay Muslims in a similar situation did little to alleviate their distress.

Within such a context, Yoesuf's strategy has been to shift the focus of discussion to make it more empowering: as opposed to talking about "our problems as Muslim homosexuals," we talked about "the problem of Islam and homosexuality," thereby shifting the focus from individuals to the broader structures that shape our lives. This shift in focus resulted in a kind of emotional distance where gay and lesbian Muslims involved in the discussion groups could see their own lives as part of the broader contexts of Islam and homosexuality. Moreover, these discussion groups generated great material to reflect upon by Islamic theologians and social workers during the study days.

Throughout the last three years Yoesuf has invited theologians, social workers and humanists to discuss the subject of Islam and homosexuality. These discussions have been meant to inform everyday discourse on homosexuality and Islam; hence, the public was also invited to participate. Among the Muslim scholars that have been invited are the following: the founder of the Dutch Muslim Counsel, Mr. A. A. Madoe; a well-known Muslim Dutch publicist, Ms. S. A. Sattar; Dr. Prof. Farid Esack from South Africa; Imam M. Khatib from Syria, Dr. Gazala Anwar from the US/New Zealand; and Dr. Mobayyed from Ireland. International presence was important in order to move the discussion beyond national interests and local power relations between different groups. In addition to these Islamic scholars and community leaders, social service providers were in attendance from such organizations as the Dutch Refuge Organization and the Netherlands Institute for Health Promotion and Disease Prevention.

In total, five Study Days were conducted on the following topics: homosexuality and the mercy of Allah; homosexuality between Islamic thought and human rights; Islam, homosexuality and the media (the tension between text and reality); Islam, homosexuality and migration; and homosexuality between disease and proclivity. Many key points were raised. First, we discussed the difference between how Islam understands homosexuality based on the Koran, and Western conceptions of the term. *Liwata* is a concept that is used by Muslims and can be compared to the idea of sodomy. The concept of homosexuality does not contain an element of "rape," which can be the case in *liwata* or sodomy (Yoesuf Foundation, 1999a). A second key point was the important role of errors in mediatic reporting, which could have inflammatory consequences (Yoesuf Foundation, 2000). Another key point surrounded the need to tackle the issue of migration, Islam and homosexuality. Yoesuf's strategy in this regard has been to support the importance of Islamic values, while fostering an understanding of homosexuality.

Another key point arose from the last Study Day on the topic of "Homosexuality between disease and proclivity." While many Muslims define homosexuality as a disease, "enlightened" members of the community see it as acquired behaviour that can be changed with the proper "remedy." For this view, Muslims do not find support in Islamic texts, but in outdated Western ideas. Clearly, a significant consequence of such a view is that homosexuals are seen as being "faulty" in some way.

A final key point arose from our discussions of research conducted by the Yoesuf Foundation in co-operation with Fontys School for Higher Education (Bajramovic, Chajia, Pham & Philips, 2000). The main conclusion of this study was that more basic information about homosexuality from an Islamic point of view is needed in order to ensure that social services are more responsive to the needs of gay and lesbian Muslims.

In short, these Study Days provided an opportunity for knowledge-sharing among local and international key players concerned with the common cause of Muslim homosexual emancipation. Information collected from these Study Days was then presented in the context of another activity that specifically addressed homosexual men and women from an Islamic background. Workshops and lectures were given world-wide to obtain feedback from people in other countries about Yoesuf's work. The results of these endeavors will come together in a book on homosexuality and Islam, and in a conference where a culturally-specific emancipation model will be presented.

Yoesuf conceives of its activities from an empowerment perspective that recognizes the need to work on a variety of levels. In this regard, we have relied on the "rivers model," created by the Yoesuf discussion group, to construct our activities. Concretely, this means that the results of discussion groups and workshops are seen as a stream that flows into study days, which are rivers that flow into a bigger river, which is the book on Islam and homosexuality based on the results of study days. This big river digs its way into the ocean, which symbolizes the broader social change of homosexual emancipation within Islam.

ORGANIZING STRATEGY ADOPTED BY YOESUF

Underlying our organizing efforts on Islam and homosexuality is a strategy premised on the notions of emancipation and solidarity. This strategy is firmly rooted in an understanding of religion and an attempt to find dignity within existing scriptures. With this strategy, we aim to achieve emancipation in the long-term. It will become clear in this discussion that this strategy is based on emancipation as understood for a specifically Muslim population living in a predominantly non-Muslim context.

There appear to be four types of strategies adopted by those working on religion and homosexuality. The first strategy is to reject religion and religious institutions in order to emancipate homosexuals and sexual expression. The second strategy is to seek shelter in religiosity and to avoid social contact, especially with other homosexual people, in order to try to not be homosexual. The third strategy is to seek emancipation by reinterpreting religious statements on homosexuality. For example, this sometimes translates into beginning a new church or joining a new doctrine in a certain religion. The fourth strategy is to leave scriptures as they are while at the same time looking for a way to value the dignity of homosexual men and women in the context of this existing religion.

Currently, various organizations are involved in the subject of Islam and homosexuality. Examples of these organizations are: Al-Fatiha, a multi-ethnic group based in North America and the UK; Homan, an Iranian group; IPOTH, a Turkish group based in the Netherlands; and Kelma, an Arab group based in Belgium and France. In practice, these organizations follow one of the four above mentioned strategies. Some of these organizations are ethnic or national specific, while others operate worldwide and on a multicultural basis. The Yoesuf foundation is trying to create long-term change, and this is why we outreach to Muslim homosexual people and various religious leaders inside and outside Europe. While being the most difficult and the less used by organizations concerned with Islam and homosexuality, the fourth strategy is the one adopted by Yoesuf. Our strategy is to leave aside holy texts as they are, and to focus instead on the changeable aspects of the Muslim community's ideas on homosexuality. We find this strategy to be appropriate when attempting to address the many actors contributing to aggression and intolerance towards homosexuality.

Dutch newspapers have reported violence against homosexuals in certain gay meeting places. The *National Volkskrant* and the *Dutch Gay Krant*, for example, featured several articles on this subject throughout May 2001. According to these articles, a large percentage of the people exhibiting aggression and intolerance towards homosexuals are people of Moroccan and Turkish origins. This has led in the media to an association of intolerance towards homosexuals with Islam.

Some analyses have attempted to understand why some migrants have problems with homosexuals; in several *National Volkskrant* articles, the social and economic situations were given as a reason for why these mostly young, male migrants with poor prospects for the future commit these acts of aggression; it was suggested that they find in homosexuals scapegoats on whom they can ventilate their frustrations. Another analysis advances the idea that this aggression against homosexuals is a symptom of repressed homosexuality on the part of some of these young men. Within these latter analyses, the association of intolerance with Islam was more nuanced.

Research undertaken by Yoesuf demonstrates that the negative attitude towards homosexuality of some Moroccan Muslims in Europe is based on three pillars. The first pillar is the perception of homosexuality as sodomy. The second pillar is the idea that homosexuality is a type of illness or at least a learned behaviour. The third pillar is the religious prohibition on sexual activities between people from the same sex. Only the third pillar comes from holy texts and on its own forms no reason for aggression or homophobia if it is not accompanied by the other pillars. This is why Yoesuf has chosen to work on changing the first and second pillars and to leave the third as is.

The Foundation has undertaken the challenge of changing the idea that homosexuality is a disease that can be transmitted and has been hard at work showing the difference between sodomy and homosexuality. We have depended in these actions on mainstream Islamic literature written by recognized writers in order to reach an audience within the Islamic community. The strategy described so far in this paper has worked well with Muslim religious leaders in the Netherlands and is still gaining success inside the mainstream Muslim community in Europe and abroad–e.g., organizations such as Islam and Citizenship, the Turkish Milli Çurus, and the Union of Moslem Morrocan Organizations in the Netherlands.

ALLIANCES IN THE WORK OF YOESUF

As frequently alluded to in this paper, alliances with other organizations and members of the Muslim community have been key ingredients in our organizing efforts. We firmly believe that long-term change is possible only with the cooperation of all concerned parties. In this regard, we have attempted to forge alliances with three main constituents: mainstream (non-homosexual) Islamic organizations in the Netherlands; non-Muslim Dutch social service providers; as well as international advocacy organizations, Muslim and otherwise.

Mainstream Islamic Organizations

The Dutch experience has taught the Foundation that creating social change on difficult issues such as the place of homosexuality in Islam, requires a general level of basic tolerance, in order to be able to speak freely on the topic. Muslims and non-Muslims alike have difficulty seeing how to bring Islam and homosexuality together from an emancipatory point of view. This is perhaps due to the restrictive religious view of same-sex relationships. In order to address this difficulty, the Yoesuf foundation has introduced an emancipation model of addressing homosexuality that is culturally appropriate from an Islamic point of view. This model focuses on setting Muslims free from elements that block their ability to cope with visible homosexuality.

Within this model that is applied to Western contexts, there are two levels of homosexual emancipation within Islam. The first is emancipation on the social level; work on this level addresses the reaction of Muslims as a minority in the West to visible homosexuality. An example on this level is the question of how Muslim families can deal with their children going to a school that has gay teachers.

The second level in this model deals with the emancipation of Muslim people who have to deal directly with homosexuality. Work on this level addresses gay men and women with Islamic background whether they identify themselves as Muslim or not. This is particularly relevant because their family, friends or colleagues may still identify as Muslim, and work on this level concerns them as well.

This model with its two levels of emancipation has been useful in forging alliances with mainstream Islamic organizations. The first level did not occasion much effort on the Foundation's part, because Islamic organizations are already confronted by visible homosexuality in the West. Our work on the second level gained success because the Foundation paid attention to the families of homosexuals. Within Islamic societies, there is much emphasis placed on the family, not the individual, as the basic unit of society. An individual's decisions are seen in light of their impact on the family. Hence, when dealing with homosexuality, it is important to work not only with the individual, but also with the family. In other words, gay/lesbian rights should not be gained at the expense of the parents or other family members of the gay/lesbian individual. Mainstream Islamic organizations remained in regular contact with the Foundation over the past three years.

Non-Muslim Dutch Social Service Providers

In addition to alliances with mainstream Islamic organizations in the Netherlands, the Foundation has sought to forge alliances with social service agencies. Over the past three years, Dutch social service providers have become familiar with the work of Yoesuf and accept it as a key community resource.

Together with the Fontys School for Higher Education, the Yoesuf Foundation has conducted a research project to explore the social service needs of Muslims dealing with homosexuality (Bajramovic, Chajia, Pham & Philips, 2000). Four graduates from the school interviewed social workers, key figures in the Muslim community and a group of homosexual Muslims. This group included 50 social service providers from organizations such as Regional Institutes for Outpatient Mental Health Care (RIAGG), and the Dutch Association for the Integration of Homosexuality–Cultural Leisure Centre (N.V.I.H. COC), the national gay and lesbian organization.

The study showed, among other things, that current services in the Netherlands do not adequately respond to the needs of homosexuals from a Muslim background. More specifically, Dutch social service providers felt limited in their interventions with gay and lesbian Muslims because these providers did not know how to deal with the central dilemma expressed by these clients: namely, the seeming contradiction between holding Muslim beliefs and practising homosexuality.

One of the study's recommendations is the need to ensure that social services respond more effectively to the needs of homosexual Muslims. Moreover, the study recommends that the Foundation focus on becoming more goal-oriented and less theoretical. To this end, the results of the study are currently being used by Yoesuf to develop a practice model that better responds to the needs of Muslim gays and lesbians, as well as their families and others in their environment. According to agreements with the Dutch Ministry of Welfare (VWS), this model will be implemented on a wide-scale.

Briefly, this model advocates for collaboration between Islamic organizations and Dutch social service providers in order to provide psychosocial support to Muslim gays and lesbians facing the dilemma of reconciling their religious roots with their sexual identity. During sessions with Dutch social service providers from VWS, Muslim clients are provided with the option of speaking anonymously with an Islamic advisor. Moreover, they are encouraged to attend Yoesuf's discussion groups. The results of the sessions with the advisor are then reported to the social worker by both the client and the Islamic advisor. The short experience that we have had with this model has shown us that clients respond well to this collaboration permitting them to reconcile their Islamic roots to their everyday existence within a Western context.

International Organizations

In the past three years, we have found it essential to collaborate with international organizations. They have provided a source of mutual support and information that has helped us to continue our work on the issue of homosexuality within Islam. Among our key collaborators are the following organizations: The International Gay and Lesbian Human Rights Commission (IGLHRC), Al-Fatiha, and Women Living Under Muslim Law (WLUML).

While not a specifically Muslim organization, the IGLHRC has been a key supporter in our work on religious intolerance of homosexuality. This organization is an international body based in California focusing on the protection and advancement of the human rights of people and groups discriminated against on the basis of sexual orientation, HIV status or gender identity.

In July 2000, Yoesuf took part in a conference organized by the IGLHRC on sexual diversity and religious intolerance, as part of World Pride celebrations in Rome. Involvement in the "Separation of Faith and Hate" conference resulted in the drafting and signing of a solidarity statement with the IGLHRC, and many other organizations interested in battling religious intolerance (International Gay and Lesbian Human Rights Commission, 2000). The "Statement of Solidarity on Religious Intolerance and Sexual Diversity" relies on the Universal Declaration of Human Rights in supporting the basic freedoms of expression and beliefs. The drafting and signing of this statement were key moments in the life of the Yoesuf Foundation because they permitted us to confirm our commitment to work in solidarity across national boundaries.

In addition to the IGLHRC, we have forged an important alliance with Al-Fatiha, an international foundation based in Washington, DC that seeks to provide a safe space and discussion forum for lesbian, gay, bisexual, transgendered and questioning (LGBTQ) Muslims and their friends. Al-Fatiha relies on Islamic notions of justice to battle homophobia and heterosexism, and to attempt to reconcile LGBTQ Muslims with their faith.

Finally, our work has also been supported by Women Living Under Muslim Law (WLUML), an international network based in the UK that attempts to provide information and support for women whose lives are shaped or governed by supposedly Muslim laws. Together with WLUML, we have collaborated successfully in offering workshops on strategies to work with the issues of Islam, sexuality and homosexuality. We offered these workshops at international conferences such as Al-Fatiha's where Muslims of various sexual orientations and ethnic origins came together.

FUTURE DIRECTIONS

At the time of writing this article, in May 2001, a documentary was shown on national television on intolerance by Moroccan youth. In this documentary an Imam–a religious figure–said that homosexuality is a disease that can be transmitted and this may result in ending mankind. In the eyes of the public, the connection between intolerance and Islam exploded. In response to the initial comments as well as the subsequent public outcry, the Prime Minister declared that there is no place for homophobia nor for xenophobia in the Netherlands.

Throughout these events, Yoesuf was called upon by the media to speak about the issues involved in this incident. As distressing as such an event may be, it represented for the Yoesuf Foundation a high point where we saw come to fruition three years of work. Our involvement in responding to this incident showed us the place of respect that the media accorded us by considering us a credible source of information on the issues involved. Moreover, we were pleasantly surprised by new alliance agreements forged with an Islamic organization called "Islam and Citizenship," as well as COC, the largest gay/lesbian advocacy organization in the Netherlands. These agreements stipulate that a national dialogue will be organized where common interests between Islamic groups on the one hand and Dutch gay and lesbian groups on the other will be explored.

In addition to these future activities, the Yoesuf Foundation is preparing the aforementioned book about the relationship between Islam and homosexuality. Currently, our plan is to publish the book in October 2001 and to launch it during an international conference. The first edition of the book will be in Dutch;[1] the book will be based on Islamic literature, contextualizing how Islam deals with social issues in general, and with homosexuality in particular. The contents of the book will include the following important aspects: a discussion of Islamic teachings and homosexuality, including a review of pertinent issues in Islamic lawmaking; a discussion of Islamic thought on homosexuality; and a description of a possible form of emancipation of homosexuality within Islam, in which a model of psycho-social support for Muslims around the issue of homosexuality will play an important role.

As evident from this article, Yoesuf has valued the importance of intervening on a variety of levels in its community organizing work. We have joined our reflection on issues during events such as the Study Days, with action such as responding to the events of May 2001. Moreover, we have intervened not only with individual homosexual Muslims and Islamic scholars, but also with social service agencies, and Muslim community organizations. Finally, our work has been based on an understanding of the interconnections between homophobia, heterosexism and xenophobia. This recognition has prompted our desire to forge alliances on both national and international levels, and with the various key players interested in reconciling homosexuality with Islam.

NOTE

1. More information can be obtained by e-mailing us at <research@yoesuf.nl>.

REFERENCES

Bajramovic, M., Chajia, H., Pham, H., & Philips, E. (2000). *Hulpverlening aan homoseksuele in de strijd tussen rede en emotie [Research of Dutch social services on homosexual people with Islamic background]*. Eindhoven: Fontys Hogescholen.

International Gay and Lesbian Human Rights Commission. (2000*). Statement of solidarity on religious intolerance and sexual diversity*. Retrieved April 1, 2001 from <*www.iglhrc.com*>.

Yoesuf Foundation. (1999a). *Homosexuality and the mercy of Allah. Report of Study-day I of the Yoesuf foundation, 6 March 1999 in Utrecht*. Utrecht: Stichting Yoesuf.

Yoesuf Foundation. (1999b). *Homosexuality between Islamic thinking and human rights. Report of the Study-day II of the Yoesuf foundation, 19 June 1999 in Utrecht*. Utrecht: Stichting Yoesuf.

Yoesuf Foundation. (2000). *Islam in the West and homosexuality: Strategies of approach. A collection of lectures given at Study-day III and IV of the Yoesuf Foundation*. Utrecht: Stichting Yoesuf.

Towards Equality Through Legal Reform: Empowerment and Mobilization of the Tongzhi (LGBT) Community in Hong Kong

Chung To

SUMMARY. The focus of this article is the author's experience as one of the organizers of a recent campaign for tongzhi rights in Hong Kong. Tongzhi in general refers to lesbians, gays, bisexuals and trangendered people, and in some cases, their supporters as well. After ten years of public education and political advocacy, the tolerance level of the general public towards homosexuality has increased. However, despite this improved atmosphere, the situation remains far from ideal. Citing the recent legal advocacy campaign as an example, this paper illustrates how the proactive approach of tongzhi activists has resulted in significant progress in the battle for equality. These efforts began with Hong Kong's first tongzhi-led campaign supporting pro-tongzhi candidates to win seats in the Legislative Council, which subsequently contributed to the formation of a Subcommittee within the new Legislative Council with a specific mandate to review the situation of discrimination against sexual minorities. *[Article copies available for a fee from The Haworth Document Delivery Service: 1-800-HAWORTH. E-mail address: <docdelivery@haworthpress. com> Website: <http://www.HaworthPress.com> © 2004 by The Haworth Press, Inc. All rights reserved.]*

[Haworth co-indexing entry note]: "Towards Equality Through Legal Reform: Empowerment and Mobilization of the Tongzhi (LGBT) Community in Hong Kong." To, Chung. Co-published simultaneously in *Journal of Gay & Lesbian Social Services* (Harrington Park Press, an imprint of The Haworth Press, Inc.) Vol. 16, No. 1, 2004, pp. 65-74; and: *Community Organizing Against Homophobia and Heterosexism: The World Through Rainbow-Colored Glasses* (ed: Samantha Wehbi) Harrington Park Press, an imprint of The Haworth Press, Inc., 2004, pp. 65-74. Single or multiple copies of this article are available for a fee from The Haworth Document Delivery Service [1-800-HAWORTH, 9:00 a.m. - 5:00 p.m. (EST). E-mail address: docdelivery@ haworthpress.com].

KEYWORDS. Tongzhi, Hong Kong, legislation, advocacy, election, Legislative Council

INTRODUCTION

Since the decriminalization of male homosexual acts in 1991, Hong Kong's Tongzhi Movement has progressed significantly. Tongzhi in general refers to lesbian, gay, bisexual and transgendered persons (LGBT), and in some cases, their supporters as well. The term literary means "comrades" in Chinese, and has become a popular reference to sexual minorities in Chinese societies, especially in Hong Kong and Taiwan, since the late 1980s.

After ten years of public education and political advocacy, the tolerance level of the general public towards homosexuality has increased. During the process of community building, such as organizing international tongzhi conferences and media events, not only has the general public become more accepting, but the local tongzhi community itself has been empowered as well. More tongzhi are willing to face the media and openly fight for tongzhi rights; the social scene and sexual space for tongzhi have also expanded. However, despite this improved atmosphere, the situation remains far from ideal. Although gay bashing is rather uncommon in Hong Kong, last year a female couple kissing on the train was bashed by another passenger. Incidents of discrimination against tongzhi continue to occur in Hong Kong.

Currently, tongzhi in Hong Kong are not content with the increased social acceptance; they also want to be legally protected and to enjoy equal status and benefits as compared with their heterosexual counterparts. The core of what has developed into a legal advocacy campaign is an anti-discrimination bill. Moreover, legal recognition of same sex partnership and equality in terms of the minimum age of consent also are on the agenda.

Although there is common ground between the tongzhi movement in Hong Kong and LGBT activism in the West, the former should be understood within its own context. In light of globalization, including globalization in LGBT politics, one should be careful not to judge the Hong Kong experience by the standards of the West. Resistance to homophobia and heterosexism take shape differently in different contexts. For example, while a GLBT pride parade may not be necessary or feasible within the context of Hong Kong, other strategies are more appropriate for the context. Citing the recent legal advocacy campaign as an example, this paper will illustrate how the pro-active approach of tongzhi activists has resulted in significant progress in the battle for equality in the context of Hong Kong.

These efforts began with Hong Kong's first tongzhi-led campaign[1] supporting pro-tongzhi candidates to win seats in the Legislative Council, which subsequently contributed to the formation of a Subcommittee within the new Legislative Council with a specific mandate to review the situation of discrimination against sexual minorities. Later on, a support letter campaign was launched and resulted in over 700 support letters flooding the Legislative Council urging equal rights and legal protection for sexual minorities in Hong Kong.

THE FIRST TONGZHI-ORGANIZED ENDORSEMENT CAMPAIGN

Since Hong Kong was returned to the People's Republic of China in 1997, the Hong Kong Government has explicitly expressed its intention to tackle the issue of discrimination through public education instead of legislation. However, new developments in recent months have made legislation a step closer to reality. New momentum was generated around the election of the incumbent Legislative Council in September 2000. Several months prior to the election, tongzhi activists realized how tongzhi's active participation in the election could potentially increase the visibility of the tongzhi population and push the tongzhi movement forward. As a result, a special working group entitled "Legco 2000 Election Mobilizing Taskforce" (the "Election Taskforce") was formed, comprising eight members, including the author of this paper. The Election Taskforce was named under the Tongzhi Community Joint Meeting, which is a coalition of approximately 16 tongzhi-related organizations.

With a population of almost seven million, it has been generally accepted that Hong Kong has approximately 350,000 to 500,000 tongzhi in its population, which represents a large constituency of voters. However, the voting power of this group had been largely ignored due to its invisibility. It was the intention of the Election Taskforce to increase tongzhi community's visibility and to consolidate tongzhi's voting power.

The Election Taskforce was quite busy during the several months leading up to the election in September 2000. One of the key activities was the production of a questionnaire for the candidates in order to identify each candidate's level of support on tongzhi issues. There were five questions in the questionnaire emphasizing the need to increase the visibility of and support for tongzhi through the provision of resources in education and social services as well as the importance of legislation in eradicating discrimination.[2] The questionnaire was sent to all 155 candidates, and approximately one third of them responded. Among those who have responded, over 70% were supportive to the cause. Based on the feedback from the questionnaire and follow-up meetings with some of the candidates, the Election Taskforce selected one candidate from each of the five voting districts for endorsement. Results of the questionnaire, along with the endorsement and analysis, were subsequently published in the *Tongzhi Voters Guide*, which was made available to the public shortly prior to the election.

It was the first time that the tongzhi community took such a high profile, pro-active approach in politics by openly endorsing tongzhi-friendly candidates, and asking tongzhi and other pro-tongzhi voters to act together as "block votes." Initially some candidates were concerned that openly supporting tongzhi causes would be an election "poison" for them, as their supportive stance might result in loss of votes from conservative voters. However, their concern was later proven to be invalid as all five candidates endorsed by the Election Taskforce won the election.

After the election, the tongzhi community hosted a thank you reception in a tongzhi bar. The media and many pro-tongzhi candidates, successful in the election or otherwise, attended. Their appearance served as an appreciative gesture to the tongzhi community, and also sent a message to the public demythologizing the "mysterious tongzhi underworld."

THE CAMPAIGN CONTINUES:
THE WORK OF THE LEGCO SUBCOMMITTEE

Following the election, as the Legislative Council began its new term in late 2000, tongzhi activists reminded some legislators about putting tongzhi issues on their agenda. In December, Legislative Council member Cyd Ho organized a public hearing regarding discrimination against sexual minorities. Other legislators, including Albert Chan, So-yuk Choy and Emily Lau, also attended the meeting.

At the end of the hearing, it was felt that many issues would need to be further explored, which could not be done without the formation of a special subcommittee. As a result, a subcommittee was formed to investigate whether there exists discrimination in Hong Kong against people on the ground of sexual orientation (the "Legco Subcommittee"). Over the next twelve months, the Subcommittee would meet several times, discussing areas of potential discrimination one by one, from education to housing, from the medical system to marriage. Because of Legislative Council's political clout, many government officials were summoned to the Subcommittee and had to respond to queries on government policies affecting tongzhi, something that the tongzhi community was not able to do on its own before.

After several meetings of the Legco Subcommittee, a public hearing was held on August 20, 2001. Several days prior to the hearing, a support letter campaign was launched, which began with an e-mail urging people to write support letters to the Legco Subcommittee. On the Thursday evening prior to the public hearing to be held on Monday, the Legco Subcommittee had received far more letters opposing homosexuality in general and legislation for tongzhi rights in specific. That evening, the author of this paper wrote an e-mail, initially to friends, contacts and lists of e-groups, asking them to write support letters to the Legco Subcommittee. Thanks to Internet technology, the e-mail was quickly spread to many. In the end, over 700 support letters were received by the Legco Subcommittee. The wide circulation and overwhelming support was beyond expectation.

At the public hearing of the Legco Subcommittee on August 20, 2001, over twenty individuals and representatives of mostly tongzhi and religious organizations expressed their views on tongzhi issues and the need to legislate, with most of the speakers supporting the cause.

In the last two efforts to introduce an Equal Opportunities Bill in 1995 and 1997, sexual orientation was just part of a larger rights campaign, and tongzhi issues, to a certain extent, just tagged along. This time, however, the tongzhi community took a much more pro-active approach and fought for its own rights. This phenomenon represented a change in attitude: Never before had there been so many tongzhi open about their sexuality, willing to face the media and speak at the Legislative Council. Emily Lau, a member of the Legco Subcommittee, was astonished by the overwhelming turnout from the tongzhi community at the public hearing. She recalled that several years ago when the Legislative Council was conducting a similar public hearing on the issue, it was almost impossible to find tongzhi to testify. As mentioned earlier, a decade of community activism on tongzhi issues had strengthened the community and had raised the levels of tolerance and awareness among the general public.

At the hearing, tongzhi activists and other representatives expressed the need for legal reform in three areas, namely the introduction of an anti-discrimination bill covering sexual orientation, same sex partnership, and equality in terms of the minimum age of consent. The core of the legal advocacy campaign is the call for an anti-discrimination bill protecting sexual minorities. Hong Kong currently has three Equal Opportunities Bills prohibiting discrimination on the grounds of gender, family status and disability status. There is no legislation, however, covering sexual orientation. Tongzhi activists have argued that legal reform is necessary in order to provide protection and equal rights for tongzhi. For example, tongzhi could be fired by an employer because of his or her sexual orientation. Many tongzhi face discrimination in their workplace, and live under tremendous fear at work on a daily basis.[3]

However, in this round legal advocacy campaign, what many tongzhi activists wanted was not merely an Equal Opportunities Bill, but a more comprehensive provision of equal rights and benefits, including the right to form families and to enjoy spousal benefits through same sex partnership. What many tongzhi wanted might not be marriage in a conventional, heterosexual way, but the spousal benefits resulting from such legal recognition. Many countries have tackled the issue by offering civil union/domestic partnership to same sex couples. Therefore, without "upsetting" the marriage system, same sex couples could be legally recognized and enjoy spousal benefits, in such areas as taxes, medical coverage, housing and insurance.

The third area regarding inequality is the minimum age of consent for sexual intercourse. Hong Kong is one of the few societies in Asia that has explicit laws regarding male homosexuality. There are no laws regarding homosexual acts between two women in Hong Kong. The law regarding buggery was first introduced to Hong Kong by the British colonial government in 1861, and the law on gross indecency in 1901. Although the Sexual Offense Act of 1967 was passed by the British Parliament, which decriminalized buggery and gross indecency between consenting adult males in private, the corresponding laws remained unchanged in Hong Kong. It was not until July 10, 1991 that a Criminal Amendment Bill was passed at the Legislative Council decriminalizing homosexual acts between two consenting males in private. Although the Bill was intended to remove criminal penalties related to buggery and gross indecency between two consenting adult men in private, several new criminal offenses were created specifically for buggery and gross indecency. Moreover, there still exists obvious inequality between male homosexual acts and heterosexual acts. For example, the minimum age of consent for male homosexual acts is 21 compared to 16 for heterosexual acts.

The overall position of the speakers at the public hearing was quite positive. One of the speakers at the public hearing was the author of this paper, who represented Chi Heng Foundation. This group, founded in Hong Kong in 1998 under a different name, became the Chi Heng Foundation in 1999. The Foundation aims to eliminate discrimination and to promote AIDS prevention through organizing and funding projects meaningful to the community. The Foundation has organized numerous activities, including the Media Awards on Tongzhi Coverage in Hong Kong and the AIDS Conference for Tongzhi Website Owners in Beijing. Chi Heng has also been an active participant in the political advocacy and legal reform campaign for tongzhi equality in Hong Kong.

Chi Heng Foundation's submission to the Subcommittee argued several points. The first point was that both public education and legislation need to be used in the battle against inequality. Moreover, while the government does not allow same sex couples to have legal recognition, it uses this lack of legal recognition as the very reason to deny them access to social benefits. The Hong Kong Government has been blaming lack of public support as a reason not to legislate, which seems ironic and illogical. It is precisely because of the existence of discrimination against sexual minorities that we need to implement legal protection for these groups. It would defeat the purpose of legal protection for minorities if the government has to wait until there is an overwhelmingly supportive public to legislate, which makes the legal protection much less needed.

It has been over a year since the formation of the Legco Subcommittee, which has explored many issues affecting the tongzhi population. Voices from the tongzhi community, opposition parties, government officials, and others have been heard. It is expected that a conclusive report will be issued in 2002, which will summarize the Subcommittee's view on whether there exists discrimination against sexual minorities in Hong Kong, and more importantly, how to respond to this situation.

Despite the improvement of social attitude towards tongzhi, the position of the Hong Kong government, preferring public education to legislation, remains unchanged. Depending on its final recommendations, the upcoming report from the Legco Subcommittee might put some pressure on the Hong Kong government to legislate. Combined with other factors such as a more supportive public opinion, advocacy from the tongzhi community and pressure from international human rights organizations, the government might in the near future decide to enact legislation protecting the rights of tongzhi.

FROM DECRIMINALIZATION TO EQUALITY: STILL A LONG WAY TO GO

It has been ten years since the decriminalization of male homosexuality in Hong Kong. The recent progressive development described in this paper represents an accumulation of years of hard work by many activists as well as the gradual change in the overall sociopolitical atmosphere. Tongzhi in Hong Kong nowadays not only want to have the right to have sex, but also the right to live free from discrimination and to enjoy equal status compared with their heterosexual counterparts. From a legal perspective, that includes reform in three areas, namely the anti-discrimination bill, same sex partnership, including the benefits behind such legal recognition, and equal minimum age of consent.

Increasingly, tongzhi activists have been taking a pro-active approach to achieving equality. The endorsement campaign of the Legislative Council 2000 Election and the subsequent events on legal reform advocacy were initiated and led by the tongzhi community itself. The empowerment and solidarity aspects in this kind of community mobilization were equally important with respect to public education and social awareness.

Despite recent progress, the tongzhi population remains far from achieving equality. The fight to equality is faced with obstacles, both externally from conservative groups in mainstream society and internally within the tongzhi community. Amid the support of tongzhi rights reflected in the public hearing session and in the support letter campaign, there exists a vocal opposing voice. As legislation for tongzhi rights becomes closer to reality, the "threat" is increasingly real for some conservative groups, which may have not previously focused too much of their efforts on opposing tongzhi activism. Some Christian churches and organizations, for example, have openly opposed legislation protecting tongzhi rights, citing moral and religious reasons. Although the opposing camp has been quite vocal and their views widely publicized, they cannot represent all Christians in society. Some of the speakers in favor of tongzhi rights at the public hearing were from religious backgrounds, including Pastor Fung Chi Wood, representatives from Catholic and Christian student groups, and a Christian women group.

Internal opposition within the tongzhi community is also present. Many tongzhi have become quite content with their newly found social and sexual space, which did not exist ten years ago. At present, Hong Kong has almost 20 tongzhi organizations, numerous exclusively tongzhi bars, discos, karaoke lounges, Internet chat rooms and, for men, over 20 saunas and bathhouses. However, the sexual and social space often means that the closet has been enlarged, but not eliminated. Discrimination still exists when tongzhi step out of the closet everyday to work and to interact with their families and the broader society. However, this aspect of tongzhi existence is not acknowledged by many, which sometimes makes community mobilization and activism more difficult.

In addition to legal reform advocacy discussed in this paper, several other trends and strategies have emerged, including the continued focus on public education and collaboration with other social movements. To a large extent, discriminatory attitudes towards nonheterosexuality are caused by misunderstanding and ignorance. During the past few years, although a larger sense of awareness of tongzhi issues in the general public has emerged, continuous efforts in public education and social awareness remain important strategies for promoting the long-term goal of acceptance of sexual diversity. Throughout the fight for legal protection, tongzhi activists have not forgotten the importance of public education, which is not mutually exclusive to the legal advocacy campaign, and has been carried out simultaneously.

Another emerging trend is the increased collaboration and strategic alliance between the tongzhi community and institutions serving other social movements, such as groups on human rights, anti-racism and feminism, service providers of AIDS prevention and care, students and youth associations, as well as organizations serving the sex industry. This process of collaboration not only increases the popular support for tongzhi causes, but also integrates the tongzhi movement into the larger social movement for acceptance and equality.

NOTES

1. The Tongzhi movement in the past was dominated by social networking and friendship building events, such as social parties and sports events. A few politically driven activities did exist before the election campaign but not on the same scale. Moreover, the movement has become wide-spread and currently includes exclusively female tongzhi groups, as well as a tongzhi Buddhist group, a tongzhi Catholic group, a tongzhi Christian fellowship, a tongzhi group for high school students (although it is il-

legal to have man to man sex for those under 21), a tongzhi university students group, among others.

2. Do you believe that tongzhi should enjoy the same basic rights in Hong Kong like the rest of the population? Do you support protecting tongzhi from discrimination through legislation? Do you support providing more resources in education and social services in order to increase the public's understanding and respect towards people with different sexual orientations? Do you agree that same sex couples should enjoy the same rights as their heterosexual counterparts? Do you agree that the sex education curriculum in primary and secondary schools should include syllabus on sexual orientation?

3. A similar Equal Opportunities Bill was introduced in 1995 and 1997, but was twice voted down. Originally, the Equal Opportunities Bill was a single, comprehensive anti-discrimination bill that covered, among other areas, sexual orientation. Due to the lack of support, the Bill was subsequently divided into three separate bills in order to increase the likelihood of passage. The Equal Opportunities Ordinance (Family Status, Sexual Orientation and Age) was introduced to the Legislative Council on July 28, 1995, but was defeated (24 to 31 votes) during second reading. Two years later on July 27, 1997, only days before Hong Kong was returned to the People's Republic of China, the Legislative Council again voted on two Equal Opportunities Bills similar to the ones defeated in 1995, including one that covered the ground of sexual orientation. Once again, it was defeated during the third reading only by 2 votes (27 to 29 votes).

A Fair Representation:
GALZ and the History
of the Gay Movement in Zimbabwe

Keith Goddard

SUMMARY. Relying on archival documents as well as the author's involvement with Gays and Lesbians of Zimbabwe (GALZ), this article traces the historical development of the gay liberation movement in that country. The author focuses on the GALZ's relationship to the media and to the state in describing community organizing efforts against homophobia. A case example of organizing is provided in order to emphasize the importance of self-empowerment and to discuss the birth of liberationist sentiments in the gay and lesbian community. *[Article copies available for a fee from The Haworth Document Delivery Service: 1-800-HAWORTH. E-mail address: <docdelivery@haworthpress.com> Website: <http://www.HaworthPress. com> © 2004 by The Haworth Press, Inc. All rights reserved.]*

KEYWORDS. Zimbabwe, GALZ, empowerment, homophobia, media, community organizing, state

In memory of Poliyana Mangwiro who fought bravely

[Haworth co-indexing entry note]: "A Fair Representation: GALZ and the History of the Gay Movement in Zimbabwe." Goddard, Keith. Co-published simultaneously in *Journal of Gay & Lesbian Social Services* (Harrington Park Press, an imprint of The Haworth Press, Inc.) Vol. 16, No. 1, 2004, pp. 75-98; and: *Community Organizing Against Homophobia and Heterosexism: The World Through Rainbow-Colored Glasses* (ed: Samantha Wehbi) Harrington Park Press, an imprint of The Haworth Press, Inc., 2004, pp. 75-98. Single or multiple copies of this article are available for a fee from The Haworth Document Delivery Service [1-800-HAWORTH, 9:00 a.m. - 5:00 p.m. (EST). E-mail address: docdelivery@haworthpress.com].

INTRODUCTION

In the first half of 1995, a small, unknown group of homosexuals[1] calling itself GALZ hit the headlines in Zimbabwe when it applied for a stand at the Zimbabwe International Book Fair (ZIBF), which had as its theme that year, "Human Rights and Justice." The group's efforts and the vehement backlash from the state attracted a great deal of local and international attention from Zimbabweans, politicians, church leaders, journalists, researchers and the international lesbian and gay movement. Gay was the buzzword in Harare in cafes and bars; discussion raged on an American e-mail discussion group, Zimnet, mostly between me and homophobic Zimbabweans resident in the United States.

Although the GALZ story has been covered in some detail by the international press and various researchers and most notably by historian Epprecht (1999), the contribution of many who took part in the movement in the 1990s has not been fully highlighted. To some extent this is due to concerns about confidentiality; in another way it is a reflection of a time when writers have been at pains to emphasize the existence of black gay men and lesbian women. This article serves to balance the picture and bring to the fore the contributions of a number of men and women in GALZ between 1980 and 1999 against a background of the history as we know and remember it. A brief recap of the "social scene" will lead into a discussion of the politicization of gays and lesbians and to the birth of GALZ. The underlying belief guiding this exploration is that rendering visible the historical roots of our struggle is in itself empowering. Moreover, this exploration helps to situate the importance of GALZ's participation at the Book Fair as an exercise in banishing invisibility and fostering self-empowerment through politicized action.

HISTORICAL BACKGROUND: PRECOLONIAL TIMES TO 1980

One of the greatest strengths of the anti-gay lobby in Africa has been the absence of a proper historical record of same-sex sexual activity on the continent prior to the coming of colonialism. Murray and Roscoe (1998) have done much to collect together under one title materials that show that researchers, explorers, missionaries and general travelers in Africa did come across same-sex sexual institutions and activity in the past. Much of this anthropological commentary is sketchy and marred by the moral prejudices of times gone by but, the fact remains, homosexual activity did occur in Africa prior to the coming of "the white man." The earliest existing evidence in what is now Zimbabwe is a *Khoisan* (Bushman) painting depicting sexual activity between a group of men. Interpreting the exact meaning of the painting is difficult at this distance in time but sex is certainly very clearly depicted.

Traditional institutions in Zimbabwe where a spirit medium may sometimes be possessed by a spirit of the opposite sex, has given rise to theories that this was one way in which homosexuals were able to fit in and gain acceptance within society. Although the idea is obviously attractive to those keen to unearth examples of gay love in ancient Africa, there is no clear evidence for the assumption and, as far as the Zimbabwean scenario is concerned, it may be one of those examples of wishful thinking using historical hindsight.

Sensible deduction has been used to work out what was likely to have been the fate of the homosexual in Zimbabwe outside the influence of Christianity, capitalism and colonialism. In the case of homosexuals, no physical evidence of difference would have been obvious and Zimbabweans did not think of homosexuality as a medical condition or a perverted evil. Instead, heavy emphasis was placed on producing children.

Similarly, homosexual activity may not have been socially sanctioned but early court records suggest that, under customary law, it was considered a lesser offense than adultery. However, when it came to consensual same-sex relationships, it is clear that a chief would have had difficulty deciding to whom damages should be paid. In the case of a sixteen-year-old and his older lover, the chief probably referred the matter to the District Administrator because there was no traditional law he could use to arbitrate on the matter.

The emphasis laid on procreation in the past is clear not from documents but from social and religious practices still in place. Still today, should a Shona man or woman die without producing children, it is not possible to hold a *kurova guva* memorial ceremony at the end of which relatives beat the grave to awaken the spirit and accompany it back to the village. It is the children who call for a *bira* in which their family ancestors participate. No children, no *bira*!

The greatest step forward in the documentation of the history of homosexuality in Zimbabwe came through Epprecht (1999) finding of around three hundred trials for sodomy and homosexual indecent assault each involving two black men, which were heard before the Southern-Rhodesian law courts between 1892 and 1923. Cases began to appear before local magistrates within months of the courts opening in Salisbury–now Harare–on 10 June 1892. The indication here is that it was not homosexuality that was imported into Zimbabwe but homophobia. These cases may present a distorted picture of the past since they came to public attention when there was dissension between the parties involved but the sheer number of cases indicates the level of homosexual activity.

Colonial Times

Oliver Phillips (1999) has described extensively how the white Rhodesian state exhibited paranoid fears about African sexuality referring to it as "the black peril." Homosexuality was viewed as just one more criminal facet of the primitive savage sexual drive of the native that Victorians strongly disapproved of and did everything to stamp out (Goddard, 2002). Such was the fear that African men looked for every opportunity to look lasciviously upon or rape a white woman, stringent laws were introduced forbidding any black man even to gaze upon the naked body of a white woman (Epprecht, 1999).

Homosexual activity in Southern Africa has always been common in prisons and between migrant workers on the mine compounds. It is through the mines that the word *ngochani*, derived from other Bantu languages such as the Nguni *(ngotshana)* first began to appear in the Shona language (Epprecht, 1999). Strangely enough, there is no entry for *ngochana* (or its modern equivalent *ngochani*) in Father Michael Hannan's (1959) *Standard Shona Dictionary* although the work contains a huge array of other sexual and sexually explicit words. The word *ngochani* is closely associated with the phenomenon of temporary mine marriages, which has been well covered by authors such as Gevisser and Cameron (1995).

In the early years of the Southern Rhodesian administration, the British South Africa Company, was preoccupied with three issues, race, land and morality. The first immigration ordinance of 1903 was drawn up to facilitate the importation of native labour from neighbouring states to work the mines and although no specific mention of homosexuality was made in this ordinance, debate took place around guarding against Southern Rhodesia becoming "a dumping ground for undesirables" who were being deported from other countries.

In the 1914 Immigration Act, specific mention appears for the first time of persons convicted of sodomy or unnatural offenses being declared prohibited immigrants. This was expanded in 1954 to prohibit anyone practising prostitution or "homosexualism" from entering Rhodesia. The clause reappeared in the Immigration Acts of 1966 and 1979 and in the last revised version of 1996. But despite these harsh laws, by the 1940s, convictions for sodomy and indecent assault had virtually disappeared both because homosexual activity had been driven further underground and, by then, the courts considered such matters trivial.

The Unilateral Declaration of Independence (UDI) Period

The Rhodesia Front came to power in 1964 and in November 1965, declared unilateral independence from Britain. The UDI government concentrated on curbing black nationalist political activity, through draconian legislation such as the "Law and Order Maintenance Act" (LOMA), whilst attempting to gain international recognition by trying to convince Britain and the United States that it was defending the Christian world from infiltration by the evil of communism. There was a strong moral tone to laws of the UDI period reflective of an intention to conserve traditional values of Christian morality. The 1966 and 1979 immigration acts declared as a prohibited immigrant any person who (i) is a prostitute of homosexual; or (ii) lives or has lived on, or knowingly receives or has received, any part of the earnings of prostitution or homosexuality; or (iii) has procured persons for immoral purposes. The Censorship Act of 1967 does not mention homosexuality specifically but, nevertheless, carries a highly moralistic tone. It was this same act that the Zimbabwean state tried to use to prevent GALZ from exhibiting at the 1995 and 1996 Zimbabwe International Book Fairs.

With the isolation of Rhodesia from the mid-sixties to 1980, cultural influence from outside remained minimal. Nevertheless, there was a thriving underground gay and lesbian scene amongst middle class whites and coloureds,[2] which has never been thoroughly documented. *Illustrated Life Rhodesia* ran an article in 1977 about Salisbury's gay club, Bali Hai (Bond-Smith, 1977). Although not anti-gay, the tone is pitying and condescending. Someone is quoted as saying that "the police know about us, but leave us alone" (p. 8) and the article pinpointed the site of the club. Soon after, it was raided by the police and shut down. The general feeling of those interviewed was that they did suffer from some abnormality but that there was nothing they could do about it; none of those interviewed gave their real name.

AN EMERGING COMMUNITY:
THE GAY AND LESBIAN SOCIAL SCENE IN THE 1980s

Post-independent Zimbabwe presents a markedly different picture and the start of a determined struggle for gay pride and dignity. Stonewall had had little direct political impact on the isolated gay and lesbian community in Rhodesia but there was a sense of fresh hope and new-found freedom for everyone in the country, including gay and lesbian people.

Most of the white population, including some gays and lesbians, had left the country during the seventies. More left after the election results in March, which brought their worst nightmare, Robert Mugabe, into power. But, at the same time, young men who had fled the country to avoid the call up started to filter back.[3] One of these was David Reeler who returned from exile in 1980. He opened up a fashion shop, Zeon, in 1981, that became the focus for trendy and gay Harare. Over the next ten years, Reeler and Evan Tsouroullis were to become two of the most important influences on gay liberation leading to the formation of GALZ. Their involvement as well as that of others in the social scene is described in this section. This historical recap is important because it was through this social scene that the seeds for a more political struggle came to be sown. The social scene provided gays and lesbians with a venue to organize events that were defining moments in our history, such as Zimbabwe's first gay pride day celebration. As important is the role that the social scene played in breaking the isolation of gays and lesbians and providing us with the opportunities of meeting and eventually organizing for our rights.

The Club Scene

Tsouroullis (personal communication, 2001) describes a loose social scene of formal and informal gay and gay-friendly clubs starting, dissolving and reforming under different names. His description of the scene at The Inner Circle where his father's secretary took him in 1980, seems closer to queer politics than strictly gay identity.

> On one of my vacations from university she took me to this club in Strathaven called Inner Circle (. . .) My conservative upbringing did not prepare me for what we used to call the Freaks: Drag Queens, Druggies, boys wearing make-up and lots of jewelry, the air heavy with incense and dope. Basically, this was the first alternative scene in Zimbabwe. It was a reaction to Rhodesia; it was a celebration of a Zimbabwe where young people believed that they were now free to express themselves in any way they wanted. It wasn't a gay club as such. Such distinctions didn't seem to matter as much as they do now. We were alternative. The people who were not, we called straight, regardless of their sexual orientation.

Sarah's opened shortly before Independence and was gay-owned by Mark Baird and Gordon Campbell (who were later to open various gay clubs in Johannesburg) and run by gay men. On Saturday nights it was strictly gay, and there was no admittance unless you were known to the management or if you were accompanied by another gay or lesbian person.

Sarah's remained a hang out for gays for many years, but it lost its exclusively gay character around 1984 when Trevor Dalton took over management. Although gay himself, Dalton banned the drag queens and any overt expressions of affection between members of the same sex. This internalized homophobia from a member of the community resulted in a spontaneous boycott and was eventually one of the forces that inspired some of the gay and lesbian community to form GALZ.

Incidentally, in 1997/1998, his business flailing, Dalton tried to stage a comeback with the gay community by organizing gay nights. He cordoned off a separate space in the club! The community stayed away. In 1998, Dalton offered to sell his club to GALZ but the organization did not have the money and was looking to purchase the house it was operating from in the Harare suburb of Milton Park, which it bought in June that year.

In October 1983, a nightclub called The Zoo transformed into Hardcore, which was opened by Bill de Bois and Reeler and its DJ, James Morgan brought from Johannesburg a new style of music called Hi-NRG, which was then popular in the gay clubs in Europe and South Africa. Tsouroullis (personal communication, 2001) describes Hardcore as follows:

> Hardcore was undoubtedly a gay space, but it was open to anyone with an open mind. The Door Policy was displayed on a sign at the door: No Racism, No Rhodies,[4] No Drugs. The last of the three exclusion clauses was completely ignored. There was a lot of heavy drug taking and a lot of sex going on in the back rooms. But what made the club was the music.

At Hardcore, Tsouroullis first met those whom he describes as the Chief Dykes (Amanda Hammer and Sonia Pereira) and who, with Tsouroullis and Reeler would become instrumental in the formation of GALZ. He had already met Bev Clark and Brenda Burrel at the first pre-pride organization meetings, two women who were at the forefront of the GALZ 1995-96 Book Fair campaign. Lesbian women had already formed a group called the Monday Club, so separatist that it was rumoured that a certificate declaring you were a full-time practicing radical lesbian feminist was required for entrance.

An alternative club, The Chicken Run, was run by the more discreet Farmer Giles who disliked out-of-the-closet Reeler because he felt the latter was splitting the community. But Tsouroullis (personal communication, 2001) suggests that Reeler was simply tapping into the new mood of liberation:

> Yes, being gay was an important part of our identity, but Zimbabwe had just been liberated, or so we thought, and a lot of us did not want to be confined into one small gay space, out of sight out of mind. We wanted to be a visible part of Zimbabwe, and not hidden away on some farm out of town.

By the mid-eighties there was a strengthening of gay and lesbian consciousness but also growing tension between those who wanted to be visible and the rest who wanted to maintain a low profile. The first Zimbabwean gay pride at the Chicken Run in June 1985 very nearly did not take place:

> Firstly there was a major fight in the organizing stages between one of the more radical lesbians and the current editor of a large independent newspaper which resulted in a walkout by the women. Then there was an up-hill battle trying to get Farmer G to agree to let us have the [gay-pride] party there. He did not understand the concept of Gay Pride. He felt we were rocking the boat and drawing too much attention to ourselves (Tsouroullis, personal communication, 2001).

The Chicken Run was also the venue for Zimbabwe's first gay wedding, which caught the attention of local newspapers. There was no overt state campaign against homosexuals in the 1980s. The stories published in April 1986 by *The Herald* and *The Sunday Mail* were meant to arouse titillating curiosity such as the report on the gay wedding and "Men Invade Ladies Toilets."

The gay-wedding report was uncharacteristically neutral for *The Sunday Mail* but the following week, the paper published three letters all of them critical of the event: "Gay weddings a travesty," by Concerned Christian, "Disgusting Weddings" by someone from the white community and "Check Homosexuality" from a black writer. No letters were forthcoming from any gays or lesbians but this was more to do with apathy on the part of the community at the time than deliberate editorial policy on the part of the newspaper.

After Hardcore, Reeler opened the popular Beat Box in June 1984. Again, this was not an exclusively gay club but it was trendy. After the closure of Beat Box, Reeler continued to organize parties under the name of Black Ice, most of them held at the Park Lane Hotel. These included various fashion and cabaret shows, most including drag artists. Most importantly, Black Ice hosted the Ms. Outrageous Contest in 1986. This was the first *public* drag pageant to be held in Zimbabwe. A second pageant was held the following year.

Publications of the 1980s

In addition to the club scene, various publications helped shape the emergence of the gay and lesbian community. Beat Box, which opened for nine months, had its own magazine called *Fallout*, largely produced by Tsouroullis and his brother. It was handwritten and then typed, cut, pasted and photocopied. A gossip rag, it nevertheless contained the germs of writing on gay issues in Zimbabwe, including a review of Bronski Beat's *Age of Consent* album, which was an excuse to make a comment on the legal status of gays in Zimbabwe. *Fallout* was the first publication in Zimbabwe to talk about safer sex for gay men. At that time, AIDS was still thought of as a disease confined to homosexuals and the Zimbabwean government was in denial about the seriousness of the impending crisis.

Fallout, grew from a small, poorly produced rag to a more professional tabloid publication. It survived for just over two years. Although not directly connected, Fallout was the direct predecessor of the quarterly *GALZ* magazine produced by Bev Clarke and with which Tsouroullis was deeply involved. He was the secret friend in Dorothy's Friend's Diary (a camp commentary on anything that happened to be going on in the scene at the time), which continues today in a newsletter on the GayZim Web site. After Clarke stopped producing the *GALZ* magazine, it developed into the *GALZETTE* in 1996. The most recent GALZ newsletter, *Whazzup*, started in 1999.

LAUNCH OF THE GAY STRUGGLE

Around 1987, the clubbing scene generally fizzled out. Reeler, Ross Parsons, the late Chris Hunt and Tsouroullis formed The Pink Berets. It started out as a joke after an excess of marijuana at a dinner party. The scene was dead and Sarah's was closed to the community. Reeler had just built a house, ideal for parties and The Pink Berets decided to throw one. But there was a major change in tactics and policy. In the past, parties such as those thrown by Black Ice were very much public affairs and although organized by gay people, were gay-friendly rather than gay-exclusive. The Pink Berets decided it was time to have gay people organize parties for gay people. There was definitely a change in mood in the country and in the gay community.

Reelers' house became the venue for many gay events, including Gay Pride parties. The latter attracted much participation from the lesbians of the Women's Cultural Club (WCC), who organized great shows. The Pink Berets were solely an outfit for throwing parties and had no political aspirations whatsoever. Although these parties were well-received by gays as well as lesbians from the WCC, there was growing dissatisfaction with the quality of gay life in Zimbabwe. As Tsouroullis (personal communication, 2001) recalls:

> There was no overt discrimination against gays, and gay bashing was rare. But the homophobia and prejudice was there. And most of all, there were legal sanctions against the way men chose to love other men making us all 'unconvicted felons.' So by mid 1990, there were enough gays and lesbians in Harare, at least, who felt it was time to form some kind of organisation that would take care of the interests of gay people.

GALZ was launched at Reeler's house in mid-1990 after a series of meetings between interested parties. Reeler, Tsouroullis, Chris Hunt, Nigel Crawhill, Pereira, Sheila Stewart, Amanda Hammar, and Bev Scofield were the founding members. Reeler came up with the name, which he thought was suitably camp. The appearance of GALZ was not welcomed by everyone. Others were later to complain that GALZ was becoming too political but, as Tsouroullis (personal communication, 2001) makes clear:

> from the onset, the aims and objectives of GALZ were political, i.e., that we would fight for equality for gays and lesbians under the law. The strategies of course, have changed throughout the years. In the beginning, most of our activities were indeed social rather than political because it was felt that we could not begin to organise effectively without a strong community base. This could

only be constructed socially. In the beginning we had a hard time trying to convince many people within our own community of the need to organise. There was a lot of suspicion and skepticism. But in time the barriers were broken down. When people realized that GALZ was providing some services they could use, they gradually became more supportive. With the Book Fair in 1995, GALZ had no choice but to become more politicised and visible.

The Gays and Lesbians of Zimbabwe was the amalgamation of two groups, the Women's Cultural Club (WCC), and the men's party list of the Pink Berets. Except for a few coloureds, membership of both groups was largely middle class professional white men and women who identified as gay or lesbian. The activities of the organization over the next few months included safer sex workshops, commissioning lawyers to write articles detailing the position of homosexuals regarding the law and the joining of the International Lesbian and Gay Association (ILGA).

The constitution was drawn up by Oliver Phillips and adopted in February 1992. It reflects the cautious approach of the majority of the membership in the early 1990s. For example, Clause 2:5 states that "GALZ is constituted primarily to provide a service to gay men and lesbians but is not formed for the purposes of coercing anyone to lead a gay of lesbian lifestyle." Some discussion at the adoption meeting arose around matters of "promoting homosexuality" and the age at which someone should be permitted to join GALZ. In the end, it was decided that "members of GALZ shall . . . have reached the age of majority," that is 18. The main objective of the organization as clarified in the Constitution, reads,

> The principle objective of GALZ shall be to build an organization which is democratic and accountable and which shall strive for the attainment of full and equal rights in all aspects of life for all gay men and lesbians within Zimbabwe. GALZ will pursue this objective for all gay men and lesbians regardless of their sexual orientation or preference, race, class, gender or religion.

This became the GALZ mission statement in 1999, which was revised to include specific reference to bisexuals in 2000. The queens[5] in GALZ have repeatedly turned down the suggestion to include "transgendered" as a category. The objectives of the constitution include the establishment, maintenance and administration of a Gay and Lesbian Community Centre, which, in 1992, seemed an impossible dream.

Confronting Homophobia: GALZ and the Media

In the early nineties, GALZ faced the serious problem of not being able to reach out to the community that it claimed and wished to represent. The organization was almost entirely unknown outside a limited circle of white, professional, middle class lesbians and gay men with telephones. It was decided in 1993 that the organization would train counselors and that this service should be advertized in the national press and through radio and television. It was hoped that, in this way, the organization would become better known and that information would reach lesbians and gay men in the townships and rural areas.

Before 2000, the newspapers with the widest circulation in Zimbabwe were the state-controlled daily newspapers published in Harare, *The Herald* and its sister paper, *The Sunday Mail*. In Bulawayo, *The Chronicle* is directly equivalent to *The Herald* and *The Sunday Gazette* is equivalent to *The Sunday Mail*. All four papers have the reputation for being mouthpieces for government propaganda although *The Sunday Mail* is generally considered more extreme in its allegiance to the Zimbabwe Nationalist African Union-Patriotic Front (ZANU-PF),[6] the ruling party.

Radio, which reaches the largest audience especially in rural areas, and television are also under government control. From April 1980, the Rhodesia Broadcasting Corporation (RBC) continued its monopoly of the airwaves as the Zimbabwe Broadcasting Corporation (ZBC). Recent successful attempts by a private company, Capital Radio, to challenge this monopoly in the supreme court resulted in hasty legislation being put through parliament in 2001 which effectively barred all independent broadcasting initiatives through crippling license fees and the requirement that local and African content of all broadcasting services be at least 75% percent of the total programming. Television is also monopolized by ZANU-PF party politics. Senior programmers, in particular Happison Muchetetere, declare openly that radio and television are there to promote the interests of ZANU-PF.

In 1993, as part of the exercise of emerging cautiously from the closet, GALZ approached ZBC and asked for opportunities to appear on radio in discussion programs about homosexuality. As a result, two black members of GALZ, Mike Boaz and Tina Machida, appeared on a phone-in discussion program on Radio Two, which broadcasts in Shona. Shortly after, three other members, Herbert Mondhlani, Lee Price and myself, appeared on another popular phone-in program on Radio Three.

There were plans to appear on a morning program, Morning Mirror, on Radio One. Without explanation, the slot was canceled, and all further efforts by GALZ to access radio failed. Since then, there has been no local discussion on homosexuality that has included a representative of the lesbian and gay community. GALZ asked to appear on a religious discussion program in 2000 to discuss homosexuality in relation to the church but although the request was viewed sympathetically by the announcer, he feared losing his job if he gave the microphone to a member of GALZ.

The policy of the government-controlled print media has followed much the same path as the electronic media. In the 1980s and early 1990s, before homosexuality was placed on the national agenda in Zimbabwe, comment about homosexuality in newspapers was generally restricted to letters from religious bigots and a regular column in *The Sunday Mail*, "It's a Weird Weird World"[7] often ran serious foreign articles about successes in the international gay rights movement.

In 1993, in an attempt to advertize the help-line of its counseling service, GALZ submitted an application to *The Herald* to include an advert in the classifieds column of the paper. The application was rejected on the grounds that *The Herald* is a "family newspaper and does not run contact adverts for sex." All attempts to persuade *The Herald* that lesbian and gay people too come from families, were to no avail. *The Herald* sought an opinion from the Advertising Association of Zimbabwe (AAZ), which stated that since homosexuality was illegal in Zimbabwe, *The Herald* could not run such advertisements. GALZ pointed out that homosexuality was not illegal, only certain sexual acts were proscribed by law and that other services, like massage parlors were frequently advertised in the paper. *The Herald* refused to alter its stance. Ironically, in 1999, GALZ started advertising in the new independent newspaper, *The Daily News* and, to date, has met with no resistance from the AAZ, and does not expect to. For a short while, GALZ managed to run its advert in the classifieds column of *The Daily Gazette*. However, after the first appearance of the advert, the wording was changed by the newspaper; the words gay and lesbian were removed so that it was not possible to tell that this was a specialized service intended for the gay and lesbian community.

Institutionalized Homophobia: GALZ and the State

As has been briefly alluded to so far in this article, the State has been less than supportive of GALZ. In this section, I highlight two overt examples of homophobia confronted by our members. More specifically, I discuss the events of 1994[8] leading to a meeting with the Minister of Home Affairs; I also discuss the adoption of an anti-gay ZANU-PF policy.

On January 23, 1994, a *Daily Gazette* reporter who had come across the advertisement for GALZ counseling services in the paper's personal column, phoned the GALZ counseling help-line. He asked to interview someone about GALZ as he intended to flight a story in the following morning's edition. The GALZ counselor, Lee Price, agreed to contact other GALZ members for a group interview with the reporter later that day. In the afternoon, two *Daily Gazette* reporters met and interviewed a small multiracial group of gay men and lesbian women representing GALZ.

During the evening, an unidentified man called using the help-line number and threatened Price saying that it was illegal to be gay in Zimbabwe and if she persisted in promoting homosexuality here she would be deported. The caller was later identified as a staff member of the *Daily Gazette*. The following day, *The Daily Gazette* ran a headline article declaring "POLICE WARN HOMOS–Net is closing in." The article quoted then Minister of Home Affairs, Dumiso Dabengwa, as saying that homosexuality is illegal in Zimbabwe. A social meeting of GALZ members to be held on January 30th was publicized in the same article. The meeting had to be canceled because of fears of a police raid. Over the next few days, and a first for the community, letters supportive of GALZ and the lesbian and gay community were published in the letters column of the same paper.

On January 26th, GALZ representatives met with *The Daily Gazette* senior editor. He was informed in no uncertain terms by Burrel that the word "homo" is considered highly derogatory, that the behaviour of his reporters was unprofessional and that the contents of the article were inaccurate and misleading. On the following day, *The Daily Gazette* published an editorial under the title "State urged to open dialogue with gays," which feebly attempted to make amends for the damage and offense it had caused.

As a follow up, three members of GALZ, Burrel, Herbert Mondhlani and me, met with the Minister of Home Affairs at the offices of the Zimbabwe Project.[9] Dabengwa assured the GALZ delegation that he had been misquoted by *The Daily Gazette* and that he had not called for police to arrest lesbians and gay men. When asked about the possibility of any future police intervention in the business of GALZ, the Minister responded cautiously by saying that the organization was free to go about its business so long as it stayed within the law. Finally, he requested that the meeting be kept confidential. Shortly after, the Minister appeared on national television where he stated that he had met with members of the Gay and Lesbian Organization and that it was government policy to root out such evils that were foreign to Zimbabwean culture. GALZ, understandably, felt deeply betrayed. This homophobic state response was also apparent in an address by the Home Minister published on January 11th, 1995, in *The Herald*, in which he assured the Zimbabwe Council of Churches that as far as the Government was concerned, homosexuality was "abhorrent" and should be banned.

At play in these state responses is the reliance on the old and tired argument that homosexuality is foreign to Zimbabwean culture and that it is imported from the West. A *Sunday Mail* editorial published on January 15th, 1995, warned of the pernicious influence of the West, specifically as it relates to literature about "perverted sex"–homosexual–that could fall into the hands of children. This editorial was followed on January 22, 1995, by an article in the same newspaper on the attempt by William Courson of The Magnus Hirschfeld Centre for Human Rights in the United States to take the Zimbabwean government to the African Court of Justice for violations against homosexuals. The article outlined Courson's arguments in some detail but the paper revealed its underlying intention that painted Courson as a white, foreign pervert interfering where he had no business and where he was not wanted. Courson withdrew the case at the request of GALZ who argued that local remedies had not been exhausted, a prerequisite before bringing any case before the African court.

Shortly after, on February 3, 1995, *The Chronicle* Editorial provided the strongest indication at that time that government had adopted a strong anti-gay policy. This time it was the words of Mugabe himself in a speech delivered on his opening of a new hospital, where he assured the nation that his government will protect people from the abominable and destructive ideas put forth by those lobbying for the rights of homosexuals and prostitutes. The editorial continued with what has become a familiar rallying call of the Zimbabwean government: homosexuality being loathsome and abhorrent to all Zimbabweans, an importation imposed by western perverts sneaking in under the guise of human rights. Zimbabweans were to be alerted and protect their children. There were no personal life-style stories of lesbian and gay people being reported except for one article *in The High Density Mirror* of March 1994. It talked sympathetically about the plight of a young gay black man in the townships. He was not connected to GALZ and his identity has never been established.

ORGANIZING AGAINST HOMOPHOBIA: THE BOOK FAIR CRISIS

The events discussed above provided GALZ with the opportunity to become aware of institutionalized homophobia in state responses to the newly-nascent gay and lesbian movement. The Book Fair crisis referred to at the beginning of this article provided an even more concrete confrontation between GALZ and the state. The Book Fair crisis also provided GALZ its first opportunity to receive support from outside the gay and lesbian community, not only in Zimbabwe, but also from outside sources.

The decision to enter the Book Fair came after the end of a road. The state had effectively silenced us and it was impossible to advertise the counselling service. To add insult to injury, we were reading anti-gay propaganda in the papers, which was clearly a strategy to discredit the white community as morally corrupt and perverse. At an executive committee meeting in January 1995 Burrel suggested that as the theme for the 1995 Book Fair was "Human Rights and Justice," GALZ should apply for a stand. It was an act of desperation, aimed at reaching out to a few interested by-passers. Without realizing it, we had set ourselves on a path that would turn the tide of gay and lesbian history in Africa.

The minutes dealing with the preparations for the 1995 Book Fair show the fears and cautious self-censorship within the committee. The organization had decided to ask for a stand in a corner of the Book Fair above which would be a bold sign saying "information to be given only to people over the age of 18." The stand was to carry HIV and AIDS information of a general nature, application forms and two pamphlets, one in English and in Shona debunking myths about homosexuals, the other about homosexuality and the law. There was also a flier in English and in Shona advertising the GALZ counselling service.

The decision to enter the Zimbabwe International Book Fair had resulted in huge division within GALZ between members who saw this as a sensible move towards being more open and public and others who did not wish GALZ to rock the boat. As a solution, it was decided that the membership should be polled. Eighty-six percent agreed that GALZ should enter the Book Fair. The executive committee called an emergency meeting where the members resigned en masse and the organization was left in the hands of the four-member Book Fair task force (Burrel, Clark, Tsouroullis and myself), which, under the terms of the constitution, barely carried the mandate to continue. Looking back on it, I do not know how we managed the stress and conflict. There were major areas of confrontation: such as between the Book Fair and GALZ, between the two factions within GALZ, between GALZ and the government represented by the Department of Information of the Ministry of Home Affairs.

On January 27, 1995, GALZ sent in its application to participate in the Zimbabwe International Book Fair and the Freedom of Expression and of the Press *indaba,*[10] which was to be opened by the President of Zimbabwe, Mugabe. Following receipt of our application, the Book Fair called GALZ to a meeting with the Executive Director, Trish Mbanga. We were handed a letter (dated February 3, 1995) by an extremely anxious Mbanga, who must have known that she was on extremely shaky ground. The letter stated that:

> Our choice of human rights as the theme is aimed at addressing the lack of basic human rights which affect millions of people throughout Africa and particularly the appalling conditions applying to women and children. We do not wish to see the focus removed from these vital issues. Regarding the Indaba–here again we feel that issue "Freedom of Expression and of the Press" is one that affects the majority. The programme has been clearly defined to address these issues and a debate on sexuality is not within the terms of reference.

We left the meeting disappointed but resigned to the fact that our application had been turned down. However, upon further reflection I found the letter untenable and wrote a reply that I showed to the seasoned anti-apartheid activist, Norma Kitson, who suggested a number of improvements. The final version pointed out the unfairness of excluding a group simply because it was unpopular with the authorities:

> Saying that it is possible to choose to highlight only those human rights causes which are popular, comfortable and safe invalidates the underlying principles of all human rights movements. If our theme had been socially acceptable, there is no doubt that we would have been encouraged to participate in all aspects of the fair.

The letter ended with a suggestion from Kitson:

GALZ accepts that the ZIBF has the choice whether or not it wishes to allow GALZ to participate in ZIBF 95; GALZ has the choice it make it generally known that the ZIBF considered a gay organisation unsuitable for inclusion in its human rights programme.

Parts of the four-page letter were read out at a meeting of the ZIBF Board of Trustees by Roger Stringer. The board was divided on the issue but decided to uphold the ban. Two trustees, Barbara Keane and Sue McMillan, promptly resigned in disgust. Except for sympathetic letters to the press, it was the first time that GALZ had enjoyed any concrete support from outside the community.

Later that month, I attended a workshop on Freedom of the Press in Johannesburg South Africa. I was aware that the Director, Hugh Lewin was an honorary trustee of the Book Fair and that he was likely to be sympathetic. I met Lewin in March and he handed me a letter that he had written to Mbanga stating:

As an honorary trustee and prospective visitor to this year's Book Fair, I must urgently express my gravest concern at the reported suggestion that ZIBF is considering banning a GALZ stand.

Surely there's a mistake. The organizers of a Book Fair with the theme Human Rights and Justice cannot be the same people who are negating those very rights. The two are self-contradictory. At a meeting between Lewin and Mbanga in March of 1995, Lewin made it clear that there was a possibility of a boycott by South African publishers if permission for GALZ to exhibit was denied. Mbanga sought legal advice when she returned to Harare and requested a copy of the GALZ constitution, which was duly provided. Mbanga was now in a difficult position. On the one hand, she feared the Book Fair might be closed down by a government that was already suspicious of the fair's free nature; on the other hand, a boycott by South African publishers might easily have led to the collapse of the fair and its removal to South Africa.

In April, Mbanga informed GALZ in writing that the association would be permitted to have a stand at the fair. However, this permission was rescinded on July 24th when GALZ received a fax from the Book Fair accompanied by a letter from Bornwell Chakaodza, Director of the Ministry of Information, which stated that

The government is dismayed and shocked by the decision of the Book Fair Trustees to allow the so called Gays and Lesbians Association of Zimbabwe (GALZ) to participate in the Zimbabwe International Book Fair (ZIBF) . . . The government strongly objects to presence of the GALZ stand at the Book Fair which has the effect of giving acceptance and legitimacy to GALZ . . . Whilst acknowledging the dynamic nature of culture, the fact still remains that both the Zimbabwean Society and Government do not accept the public display of homosexual literature and material. The Trustees of the Book Fair should not, therefore, force the values of gays and lesbians onto the Zimbabwena culture.

Morrison, a member of GALZ, appeared shortly before lunch time saying that he had attended the Freedom of Expression *indaba* and had stood up and stated that GALZ had been banned from participating at the Book Fair. The chair of the session attempted to say that the ban was not Book Fair business but it was clear that he would not be able to proceed. Nadir Gordimar, a South African novelist and Nobel Laureate, stated that it was unpardonable that an *indaba* on freedom of expression should be taking place under the auspices of a fair that had banned an organization from participating. She called for a protest to be written and lodged with the Book Fair. This letter was written, along with an official statement from GALZ. Later that day at the Freedom of Expression *indaba,* the statement was read out and adopted by a majority of those present. Trudy Stevenson, then of the Forum Party, expressed her solidarity.

Lewin had arrived in Harare and I had hoped that he might be able to change the decision of the fair. He told me that he had been informed by Mbanga that there had been a directive from the President and that there was nothing that could be done, especially at this late stage. He said the Book Fair had decided that the booth should remain but that the GALZ sign would be removed and that it would revert to a Book Fair stand. GALZ members were prohibited from staffing it. The Book Fair would use the stand to put up all correspondence between itself and GALZ relating to the saga, including the banning notice. Luckily for GALZ, the stand across the way from the abandoned booth, the "shrine," was not occupied and so members of the Book Fair team occupied it and surreptitiously gave out brown paper envelopes with GALZ literature inside. When this information reached the media, people started to flock to "see the homosexuals" and get copies of the literature.

On Wednesday evening, the president of Zimbabwe, Robert Gabriel Mugabe, was due to open the fair. At the meeting the previous Sunday it had been decided that other exhibitors should be asked to put up signs protesting GALZ's exclusion from the fair. These were distributed on Wednesday morning, the day Mugabe was to open the fair. In the early afternoon, the ZANU-PF youth brigade descended on the fair and tore down all the notices of protest. Sue McMillan of Collins Press publishers and one of the trustees who had resigned in protest against the banning of GALZ refused to give up her sign. She was roughly pushed aside and the sign was seized.

Later in the afternoon, the President toured the fair. Roger Stringer positioned himself in front of the GALZ shrine waiting for the opportunity to show the president its contents, which, by this stage, carried a bowl of flowers from a sympathizer. But Mugabe was carefully steered away. The President later issued his opening address which contained the first of his many outbursts against the lesbian and gay community. It was broadcast on national television and reported on in *The Herald* the following day. Owing to the state stamp down, GALZ had failed to get even a counselling advertisement in a newspaper and so, ironically, it was Mugabe who launched the gay rights movement publicly in Zimbabwe. Homosexuality was the talk of the town and, from Thursday, young black men and women crowded around GALZ members at the empty stand opposite the shrine. Many were hostile, some sympathetic, others just curious.

On Saturday, the last day of the Book Fair, GALZ members ended the campaign with a celebratory meeting at the house of Lynde Francis. For the first time, virtually every person present was black. In February 1992, when I joined GALZ, the membership was still small and predominantly white although the split was equal between men and women. Andrew Morrison had recently quit his position as a member of the executive committee over what he saw as slowness on the part of GALZ to include blacks. At the celebratory meeting, one young man, Peter Joaneti, said "it is time for us to fight for our rights." Lynde Francis, also clearly elated, said that it was clear that there had been an internal revolution within GALZ and that the black community had clearly staged a successful coup.

Thus, following the events of the 1995 Book Fair, homosexuality was placed firmly on the national agenda in Zimbabwe. As importantly, the face of homosexuality in public perception was no longer seen to be just white, and, therefore, not so easily dismissed as a foreign scourge to be weeded out of Zimbabwean culture. However, with homosexuality firmly on the public agenda, attacks from the state intensified. On Heroes Day in August 1995, Mugabe referred to lesbians and gays as "worse than dogs and pigs" and tried to instigate a witch-hunt encouraging people to arrest and hand over gays and lesbians to the police. In September 1995, the parliament of Zimbabwe fully endorsed the attitude of the President. During the debate, Member of Parliament, Anias Chigwedere said:

> The whole body is far more important than any single dispensable part. When your finger starters festering and becomes a danger to the body you cut it off . . . The homosexuals are the festering finger.[11]

The clear message given to Zimbabweans and in particular the Zimbabwean police force was that lesbians and gay men could be harassed with impunity. This was certainly our experience to date, but even more so in 1996, when GALZ once again decided to join the Book Fair. In 1996 the government once again tried to ban GALZ from exhibiting at ZIBF. GALZ took the Chairman of the Board of Censors and the Minister of Home Affairs to court. On July 31st, 1996, the High Court declared the ban "null and void and of no force or effect."[12] Government appealed against the decision but the Supreme Court upheld the ruling on August 2nd, 1996.

On July 23rd, 1996, *The Herald* reported the president of a self-styled traditional group, Sangano Munhumatapa as threatening to raze down the stand even if it means going to jail. Two days later, GALZ issued a statement denouncing government threats and calling on the police to do its constitutional duty and provide protection to members of GALZ at the fair. This was met with a statement that appeared on July 27th, 1996 from ZANU-PF Harare Province Publicity Information Secretary, Tirivanhu Mudariki. The Secretary warned GALZ that if it should exhibit at the Book Fair, that the Party would mobilize all of its members against it.

Fearing the eruption of violence, the Executive Director of the Book Fair, Trish Mbanga, approached the Commissioner of Police to request protection at the Book Fair. She was told that gays and lesbians have no right to help from the police if they are attacked. The call for police protection was reiterated by the GALZ Administrator on August 1st, but this was to no avail. Indeed, on the evening of August 1st, Poliyana Mangwiro, an outspoken GALZ activist who had been at the GALZ stand during the day, returned to her home in Marondera and was met by an angry crowd from the ZANU-PF Women's League who threatened her life. Clearly there was no point in reporting the matter to the police. GALZ provided her with refuge in Harare and with transport to return to her rural home for a few weeks until the storm had blown over.

With no assistance from the police, GALZ was forced to employ the services of a security company to provide protection for GALZ members at the GALZ stand. On August 3rd, the last day of the Fair, the GALZ stand was attacked by a mob identified later as coming from Sangano Munhumutapa. Luckily, GALZ members at the stand received a tip off and were able to make a timely tactical withdrawal.

As apparent from the preceding discussion, the experiences of GALZ at both Book Fairs were indicative of the homophobic and heterosexist climate in Zimbabwe at the time that the organization was beginning to express itself politically. However, in the face of state reprisals and the lack of support expressed by many other NGO's, GALZ did secure the support of people outside the organization.

CONCLUSION

It is now nearly eight years since GALZ peeked its head out of the closet. Today, the association is hardly recognizable from what it was in the past. From a virtually exclusively white membership, GALZ now draws most of its members from younger black men in the townships. Very few women join the organisation because of problems women face in gaining access to public space–but even this is changing. GALZ now has a banner advert in the telephone directory; this, combined with the freedom to advertise in the independent press means that the association has no problem in making its counselling services available to all.

The membership of GALZ had grown from 70 in 1992 to 349 in December 1999, virtually all of the membership was black. Over the next year, GALZ will expand and decentralise through the setting up of independent Affinity Groups in ten centres outside Harare. Each of these groups will be serviced by two counsellors who, in liaison with the Health Officer at the GALZ Centre will tend to the health and well-being of members, including those members living with HIV or AIDS.

During the Book Fair crisis, other nongovernment organisations accused us of being too confrontational. Their idea was to gradually woo government to become more open and democratic. GALZ disagreed with this strategy: we had a right to exhibit and government had no right to ban us. Today, we are vindicated. With government reneging on any promises that threaten its power base, most nongovernmental organizations (NGOs) now see themselves as part of the national crisis fighting for change. But did we take the right path? On reflection, it might have been wiser for us to have tackled the courts first, but now there is no going back. Gay and lesbian people are becoming firmly embedded in civil society and one member of parliament, Tendai Biti is on record as having spoken up in favour of the inclusion of sexual orientation in the nation's next constitution.

In 2000, GALZ changed its slogan from gay and lesbian rights are human rights to sexual rights are human rights. This was an attempt to get all Zimbabweans to recognise that they have a sexuality and a right to express their sexuality as well as responsibilities not to harm others. As this article goes to press, a two-day seminar being organised jointly by GALZ and Southern African HIV/AIDS Information Dissemination Service (SAfAIDS) is being planned for April to which over 30 NGOs throughout Zimbabwe are being invited to attend. It is expected to be a full house.

Since 1995, the basic policy of GALZ has been to turn apparent defeat into triumph. This positive attitude stems from the pride we have in ourselves and the confidence and determination that we will succeed in normalising the position of LGBT people in society. Our example has already started to inspire groups in Namibia, Botswana and parts of East Africa to take up the struggle. We have proven that it can be done.

NOTES

1. The word homosexual was invented around 1869 as a medical term to define same-sex sexual attraction. I use the word cautiously here to define same-sex attraction bearing in mind that it is intended to refer to European expressions and not African ones.

2. People of mixed race in Zimbabwe refer to themselves as coloured.

3. The popular phrase for people leaving the country to avoid the war was "taking the chicken run." Many left because they did not wish to defend the racist Smith regime. Ironically, The Chicken Run night club became one of the most important venues in the emergence of gay pride.

4. "Rhodie": short for Rhodesian but more typically describing a stereotyped white character holding homophobic, sexist and racist beliefs.

5. Transgendered people in Zimbabwe prefer to refer to themselves as queens.

6. During the first half of the 1990s, an independent daily paper, *The Daily Gazette*, ran for a few years until its demise around 1995. A weekly paper, *The Financial Gazette*, more liberal in attitude still exists. The radical *Zimbabwe Independent* started in May 1996 and *The Daily News* started publishing at the end of March 1999 and now has the largest circulation in the country.

7. To quote a typical example, on 26 November 1994, the paper reported on an alleged fashion for cross-dressing in Japan under this column.

8. The details of this event are drawn principally from a letter by a GALZ executive committee member, Brenda Burrel, to Graeme Reid of the Gays and Lesbians of Witwatersrand (GLOW), March 28, 1994.

9. The meeting was arranged by Paul Themba Nyathi, then a personal friend of Dabengwa with whom he was meeting for lunch. It as felt that the Minister would not agree to meet GALZ representatives officially so the GALZ delegates simply dropped in during the lunch appointment.

10. *Indaba* is a traditional institution whereby men (and a few women acting as "honorary" men) meet and discuss affairs relating to the village, e.g., a barren woman that needs to be returned to her village, the building of grain huts etc.

11. Parliamentary debates, 28 September 1995, col. 2779.

12. Ruling In the High Court of Zimbabwe, Case H.C. 6482/96.

REFERENCES

Bond-Smith, S. (1977, January 20). Salisbury's gay club is alive and flourishing. *Illustrated Life Rhodesia*, 8-9.

Epprecht, M. (1999). Homosexual "crime" in early colonial Zimbabwe (1892-1923). *The Avid Queer Reader, 1* (1), 22-24.

Gevisser, M., & Cameron, E. (1995). *Defiant desire: Gay and lesbian lives in South Africa*. New York: Routledge.

Goddard, K. (2002). The deployment of sexuality in the building of the nation state in Zimbabwe. GALZETTE, *1*, 4-10.

Hannan, M. (1959). *Standard Shona dictionary*. London: Macmillan Publishers.

Murray, S.O., & Roscoe, W. (1998*). Boy-wives and female husbands: Studies in African homosexualities*. New York: St. Martin's Press.

Phillips, O. (1999). *Sexual offences in Zimbabwe: Fetishisms of procreation, perversion, and autonomy*. Unpublished doctoral dissertation, Cambridge University, Boston, Massachussets.

Index

For Product Safety Concerns and Information please contact our EU
representative GPSR@taylorandfrancis.com Taylor & Francis Verlag GmbH,
Kaufingerstraße 24, 80331 München, Germany

Batch number: 08169151

Printed by Printforce, the Netherlands